LEGENDS OF UNITED

The Heroes of
the Busby Era

DAVID MEEK

First published in Great Britain in 2006
by Orion
This paperback edition published in 2007
by Orion Books Ltd,
Orion House, 5 Upper St Martin's Lane,
London WC2H 9EA

1 3 5 7 9 10 8 6 4 2

ISBN 978-0-7528-8140-9

Printed and bound in Great Britain by Clays Ltd, St Ives plc

The Orion Publishing Group's policy is to use papers that
are natural, renewable and recyclable products and
made from wood grown in sustainable forests. The logging
and manufacturing processes are expected to conform to
the environmental regulations of the country of origin.

www.orionbooks.co.uk

CONTENTS

ACKNOWLEDGEMENTS

T his book has been a personal journey because writing and reporting on Manchester United through the Sir Matt Busby years represented a huge part of my working life and reliving those days has brought back many happy memories.

The trip brought back to life the many and varied characters who made United famous throughout the world and reminded me that the business of journalism is very dependent on the people we write about. So I would like to dedicate my book to all the players, and managers, who made my work possible and who over the years talked trustingly to me.

Naturally I am indebted to Sir Matt himself, the legend among legends, whose patient and perceptive management brought such wonderful players to strut their stuff on the Old Trafford stage.

I would particularly like to thank Ivan Ponting, freelance journalist and author of many books himself. I have drawn heavily on the work we did for *LEGENDS*, the magazine I edited for the Association of Former Manchester United players, now sadly out of circulation.

John Doherty, Chairman of the Association, has been, as always, a fund of information with a career launched in Sir Matt's early days and continuing as critic to the present day.

I am grateful also to the stars of the sixties like George Best, Sir Bobby Charlton, Pat Crerand, Bill Foulkes, Harry Gregg, Denis Law, David Sadler, Nobby Stiles and Alex Stepney. They all feature considerably in the book and I hope I have not abused their goodwill.

WALKING WITH LEGENDS

S upporters of every football club look back fondly on their favourite players, the stars who became legends, and the followers of Manchester United, of course, are no different.

From the moment a group of railway workers in 1878 formed themselves into Newton Heath LYR football team, named after their Lancashire and Yorkshire depot, there have been people who stood out for one reason or another.

The significant characters in those days were the enthusiasts who struggled to keep the club afloat in face of mounting debt, like the club's first full-time official, A H Albut, who at one point held a meeting lit by candles in beer bottles, because the Corporation had cut off the gas supply for non-payment of their bills.

This was an era covered by Harry Renshaw, an intrepid predecessor writing for the *Manchester Evening News*.

The stars he wrote about were players like the Welsh international brothers, Roger and Jack Doughty, and the amateur Sam Black who later became a referee. Black hit the headlines when he disallowed a Woolwich Arsenal goal against Burnley, when the goalkeeper complained that the bladder of the ball had come through a burst panel, and its erratic flight had made the ball impossible to catch. Sam Black wisely ruled that the burst ball was no longer a proper ball as the rules decreed.

I imagine Harry would have enjoyed writing the story of Scotsman Pat McDonnell, whose search for work prompted him to walk from Glasgow to Manchester, where he was given a job at the Newton Heath depot and a place in their football team.

More characters emerged after Newton Heath became Manchester United in 1902, as part of a makeover introduced by John Henry Davies, a wealthy brewer who helped save the club from bankruptcy and who became their new president.

Harry Stafford, the Newton Heath captain at their moment of crisis, and his fund-raising dog, both became local celebrities, and then, as the new-born United began to progress, with Championship wins in 1908 and 1911 as well as FA Cup victory in 1909, under manager Ernest Mangnall, the fans had some real heroes to cheer.

Billy Meredith, the Welsh wizard who insisted on playing with a toothpick in his mouth, was arguably the first celebrity footballer and certainly a great personality in his day, appearing for both United and Manchester City as well as playing a leading role along with skipper Charlie Roberts in a strike that beat the Football League's attempt to ban the Players' Union.

Sandy Turnbull, the man who scored the first goal for United at Old Trafford, following the move there from their Bank Street ground in 1910, was a popular figure before being killed in France in the First World War.

Even in the quiet years between the world wars, the crowd had their favourites like Joe Spence, so popular and well respected that if the team were having a difficult time the cry would go up: 'give it to Joe'.

Joe played over 500 League and Cup games for United and he had some doughty team-mates like the massively built Frank Barson, a blacksmith turned centre half, and Clarrie Hilditch who later became player-manager.

They were difficult times, though, as United teetered on the edge of bankruptcy again before being rescued in 1931 by another philanthropic chairman, James W Gibson. At that time they were yo-yoing between the two top divisions, and in 1934 came within a whisker of dropping down to the Third Division.

Popular though these players were, it needs especially talented players, achieving success, to make legends, and it was not until after the Second World War that we saw Manchester United begin to produce a galaxy of stars, players we rightly judge as legends through their own brilliance and through the success they enjoyed as part of a team.

The man who gave us this non-stop production of legendary players was of course Sir Matt Busby, a legend himself and in his own lifetime.

Sir Matt was incredible, the man who not only woke the sleeping giant but who kept the club, once awake, in the forefront of football for twenty-five years. In the process he built three great teams. The last one was a fitting testament to his powers because, after the Munich air accident in February 1958, he had to begin again, virtually from scratch.

His much admired team of Busby Babes was destroyed with eight players killed and others injured beyond repair, at least as professional athletes. He had lost his two coaches, Bert Whalley and Tom Curry, along with the long-serving secretary Walter Crickmer.

Yet, just ten years later Busby had rebuilt and fashioned another team of legends that won the European Cup, the first English club to become European champions. It was an incredible achievement for which I feel he and his assistant Jimmy Murphy were never really given full credit.

Never mind the practicalities of finding new players, how on earth did he find the will to carry on in face of such soul-destroying devastation?

And to think that Busby had lain at death's door himself, with such grievous injuries that, as a staunch Roman Catholic, he had twice been given the last rites. It was nearly three months before he was able to meet up with his players, after a desperate period in which he had thought he could never face a football life again.

By the time Busby was home from the Rechts der Isar Hospital in Munich and well enough to venture to Blackpool to meet up with Jimmy Murphy and his hastily rebuilt squad of players, United had reached the final of the FA Cup. A massive wave of emotion had swept Murphy's Marvels all the way to Wembley and a date with Bolton.

I vividly remember meeting Matt for the first time, when I was introduced as the *Manchester Evening News* reporter replacing Tom Jackson (one of the eight sports writers killed in the accident), in the grounds of the Norbreck Hydro Hotel, where the team were staying as they trained for the Cup. He could still only walk with the aid of crutches and was clearly in pain at times.

As if it wasn't already difficult enough for Matt to come to terms with the loss of his beloved Babes and staff who were not only colleagues but friends, he had to face an entirely new representation from the press. Most of the leading reporters who had been killed had been travelling with United all over the world and covering their exploits for a number of years, and had a close relationship with the manager.

Every one of the new boys, like my colleague Keith Dewhurst from Manchester's other evening paper, the *Chronicle*, taking over from Alf Clarke, must have been yet another painful reminder that the press had also suffered on that fateful trip home from Belgrade and the tragic third attempt to take off from Munich after a refuelling stop.

I for one certainly felt I was opening up his grief again when I was first introduced and it seemed utterly banal to start talking about football.

The Munich tragedy undoubtedly lent a mystique to the players who wore a red shirt, both before and after the crash. The tragedy certainly contributed to the club's global appeal and worldwide popularity, but it seems to me that the Busby era, with its three quite distinct but equally great teams, produced more legends than any other club in the history of the game.

Sir Alex Ferguson is going close in his twenty years as manager of Manchester United, with his own brand of outstanding footballers like Brian McClair, Peter Schmeichel, Bryan Robson, Mark Hughes, Steve Bruce, Gary Pallister, Eric Cantona, David Beckham, Roy Keane and the present crop of talent like Wayne Rooney, Ruud van Nistelrooy, Ryan Giggs, Paul Scholes and Gary Neville, but there is a mystique and an aura surrounding Busby's time, perhaps cloaked by the tragic overlay of the Munich disaster, that adds a different dimension to his players.

It certainly stands out differently in my mind after writing and broadcasting about Manchester United for close on fifty years since Munich. In my thirty-seven years as the United reporter on the *News* I missed only a handful of games and since retiring from the paper in 1995, I find myself still lending a hand with the manager's words in the match programme and contributing to the club's radio show at home games, as well as weighing in on MUTV.

I still haven't missed a European match home or away since Munich and I like to think that I am as excited by, and as impressed by, the football tyros of the present day as I was when I was first introduced to Matt Busby as one of the new kid reporters on the block, following that fateful European Cup tie in Belgrade.

I am aware that distance can lend enchantment, but there was something special about the Busby days, an aura that stemmed from the great man himself. He had a natural authority and was able to exercise it without even raising his voice. The players felt it, I know, and sometimes when they would go in to see him, perhaps to complain about being dropped or maybe wanting a pay rise or some such, they would find themselves coming out of his office apologising for troubling him.

I know that when I wrote something that upset him and he asked to speak to me, I felt I was back at school summoned to the Headmaster's study. He didn't shout – no Fergie hairdryer treatment – he just made you feel small. Mind you, I think he made the most of this natural power he had over people; I turned forty and he was still calling me 'son'.

He was a good manager to work for, though, from the point of view of a local reporter. I know this because travelling on the team bus to away games, as I did in his day, gave me the opportunity to get to know Matt, the players and everyone involved in the club.

The people I am going to write about from his first great post-war team, I got to know through interviews. I saw the Busby Babes play, tragically for such a short time, and then I had a front-row seat reporting the daring deeds achieved in the Swinging Sixties.

When I retired from the *Evening News* the Association of Former Manchester United Players made me an honorary member. I was never a savage critic, but from time to time I did have my run-ins with Busby and his players – I was eventually banned from travelling with the team – but nevertheless I was greatly touched that they had obviously forgiven me for my more critical moments.

Busby gathered special people around him, as well as exceptional footballers. They are in fact legends, and I was privileged to walk down the football road with them.

Chapter One

FOUNDING FATHER

═══

S ir Matt Busby was the founding father of the
Manchester United we know today.

Before Matt, there had been some early successes
before the First World War, but between the wars they had
done little to attract attention. The honours cupboard was bare
and the prospects, when chairman James Gibson offered him
a start in management at the end of the Second World War,
were hardly attractive.

United were £15,000 overdrawn at the bank and they did-
n't have a ground. Old Trafford had been blitzed. The pitch was
covered in glass, the dressing rooms were derelict and the
offices were located at the nearby premises of the chairman.

Matches had to be played at Maine Road on the ground of
local rivals Manchester City. There was also a shortage of players with a number of them still away in the army. Gibson knew
all about Busby, though, because as a player he had been with
neighbouring Manchester City and had impressed as their captain, as well as exhibiting instinctive command by captaining
Scotland.

Perhaps his tough upbringing had schooled him to look adversity in the eye and not shirk a difficult challenge. Life had not been easy for the Busby family. Living in the Scottish pit village of Bellshill, Lanarkshire, Matt and his three sisters were raised without a father who had been killed in the First World War.

Matt had had dreams of becoming a teacher but without a father in the house the pit was the inevitable alternative. The job brought in £2 a week and the family were looking to follow other family members to America for a better life. But while they were waiting for visas to come through, Matt found football offering him a chance.

He had been playing for one of the local teams, Denny Hibs, when Peter Hodge, the manager of Manchester City, offered him £5 a week to join Maine Road in 1928. His mother had been planning to join her sister in the States, but the chance came for Matt to try his luck in English football and so family plans were changed.

Matt probably wished that his application for a visa had come through more quickly because life at first with City was a struggle. It looked as if he wasn't going to make it, when suddenly fate played a trick that set him on his way. He had been playing as an inside forward but injuries saw him switched to wing half in the reserve team and everything clicked into place. That was *his* position and he quickly won promotion to the first team to captain City to an FA Cup final victory over Portsmouth in 1934, after they had lost heavily to Everton the previous season. His form also took him into the Scotland team and he was once again handed the captaincy. He only won one full cap – against Wales – though he did play in a string of wartime internationals.

He was admired as an attractive and stylish player as he steadily built up an appearance record of 226 League and Cup games for City before deciding to move to Liverpool in March 1936 for £8,000, to link up with Bradshaw and McDougal, a couple of fellow Scots. The outbreak of the Second World War cut short his Liverpool career, after making 118 League appearances.

Like most of his team-mates, when the war started he joined the army to serve in the 9th Battalion of the King's Liverpool Regiment. Later, because of his sporting background, he was transferred to the Army Physical Training Corps, where he became a Physical Training instructor and sergeant major, organising touring teams and matches for the troops abroad.

At the end of the war Busby was in demand. Liverpool wanted him to resume his playing career and become assistant manager to George Kay, but Gibson stepped in with an invitation for him to become manager of Manchester United. Again Busby showed himself a man with his own ideas, because while Gibson offered him a contract for three years, Busby was adamant that he wanted a longer one to give him time to put his ideas into practice.

Gibson was used to having his own way, but Busby was from a similar mould, insisted on five years and won the day.

'I got this opportunity to go as manager of Manchester United. I had a soft spot for Manchester after my City days and it attracted me,' said Matt later.

Walter Crickmer, the United secretary who had also taken on the duties of manager during the war, said at the time: 'Busby had offers from several clubs but he particularly wanted to come back to Manchester. He will build up the team and put the club right up where it belongs – at the top.'

They were prophetic words.

First though he had to prove himself as a manager. At the time he was just another soldier home from the war. The name of Matt Busby had no special magic in those days and he was about to join the cutthroat world of football management.

It did not take him long, though, to stamp his own particular style and authority on those around him. The thirty-six-year-old Busby straight away donned a tracksuit and joined his players out on the pitch in training.

Post-war this was revolutionary. As Johnny Carey, his captain in those early days, says: 'When I joined United before the war, Scott Duncan, with spats and a red rose in his buttonhole, typified a soccer manager. But here was our new boss playing with his team, demonstrating what he wanted and how to achieve it. It was unheard of in those days. Matt was ahead of his time.'

Busby also revealed an early feel and flair for the transfer market, as well as shrewdly judging a player's best position. His own experience with Manchester City had taught him that sometimes a switch of position could transform an indifferent performer into a star.

He turned his first squad of players inside out, converting Carey and John Aston, later a United coach himself and chief scout, from inside forward to fullback. They had been pedestrian as forwards, but made outstanding defenders who went on to figure hugely in Busby's first successful team.

The new boss started work in October 1945, with United lying sixteenth in the table. Such was his impact, that by the end of the season they had climbed to fourth and in his first full season, 1946–47 (with national football returning instead of it being divided into North and South) they finished runners-up, just one point behind Liverpool, the club who had also fancied him as a manager.

He had inherited quite a useful squad, though he had to wait for some of them to get back home from the services. In the meantime he made his first swoop on the transfer market to buy Jimmy Delaney from Glasgow Celtic. The football world thought he was mad to pay £4,000 for a thirty-one-year-old winger nicknamed 'old brittle bones' because of the frequency of his injuries in Scotland. He was reckoned to be finished, but he turned out to be the last piece in tshe jigsaw and proved to be a key figure in the team that brought Busby his first silverware, the FA Cup of 1948. United overcame Blackpool in the final 4–2, after a match still widely regarded as a classic.

United dominated the competition right from the start and arrived at Wembley after scoring 18 goals in five ties, an accurate reflection of their great attacking strength with a front five of Jimmy Delaney at outside right, Charlie Mitten on the left wing, Jack Rowley at centre forward, flanked by inside forwards Stan Pearson and Johnny Morris.

The full Cup final line-up was: Crompton, Carey, Aston, Anderson, Chilton, Cockburn, Delaney, Morris, Rowley, Pearson, Mitten.

The opening third round had been a tough one, Aston Villa away, and they found themselves a goal down after only 13 seconds. It was perhaps not a wise move on Villa's part because United raised their game to produce some superb football to lead 5–1 at the interval. Villa, no mean side, fought back in the rain and on a muddy pitch, to make it 5–4, but Pearson scored to give the Reds a remarkable 6–4 victory, that somehow summed up their cavalier approach to football under their new boss.

Busby's team went on to account for Liverpool 3–0,

Charlton 2–0, Preston 4–1 and Derby County 3–1 in the semi-final, with a hat trick from Pearson.

The final saw them up against a Blackpool team that included Stanley Matthews, Stan Mortensen and Harry Johnston, and there was a shock for United after only twelve minutes when Mortensen was brought down by Allenby Chilton. Eddie Shimwell beat Jack Crompton with the penalty.

Rowley took advantage of a misunderstanding in the Blackpool defence for the equaliser in the twenty-eighth minute. Mortensen restored Blackpool's lead after thirty-five minutes and they stayed in front until the sixty-ninth minute despite steadily mounting pressure. They cracked eventually, Rowley heading in a free kick from Morris for an equaliser.

United cut loose, and after Crompton had saved brilliantly from Mortensen, immediately took the lead. Crompton's goal kick was moved by John Anderson to Pearson who scored off the post from twenty-five yards. It was the killer goal and three minutes later with their opponents still reeling, Anderson scored with the help of a deflection, to give Busby a memorable 4–2 victory, for his first trophy.

The League continued to be elusive, but they were still setting a high standard of football and were consistent with it. They finished second in the League in the season they won the Cup, and although they slipped to fourth the following year, they were back in the runners-up spot before finally cracking the League by winning the Championship in 1951–52, finishing four points ahead of Spurs. The 'nearly men' had got there with basically the side that had won the Cup but with a couple of newcomers: Johnny Berry, a right winger signed from Birmingham to replace Delaney, and Roger Byrne, a dashing outside left, who would later captain the team, and become a distinguished England international fullback, following a switch of role for him by Busby. Byrne was something of an emergency switch following the defection of rebel Charlie Mitten to Colombia, to play for Bogotá and for vastly more money than he could earn in England.

The team which clinched the title was: Allen, McNulty, Aston, Carey, Chilton, Cockburn, Berry, Downie, Rowley, Pearson, Byrne.

Rowley opened that Championship season in blazing form, scoring successive hat tricks in the first two games for a 3–3 draw at West Bromwich Albion and a 4–2 home win against Middlesbrough.

They suffered early defeats against Bolton, Spurs and Preston but Portsmouth, the early front runners, fell away to leave United, Spurs and Arsenal the main challengers for the title.

The three of them were neck and neck on the last lap, and the title wasn't decided until the very last fixture. Arsenal came to Old Trafford on the final day needing to win by seven clear goals to win the Championship on goal average. Spurs had fallen behind, but it was a great finale and United did Busby proud by winning 6–1 to emerge clearly the best side. United finished on fifty-seven points with Spurs and Arsenal both four points behind. The measure of United's success lay in the scoring figures: they notched up 95 goals, way ahead of Arsenal's 80 and 76 from Tottenham.

Rowley had banged in thirty of the goals with twenty-two from Pearson and eleven from Johnny Downie.

Busby believed in attacking and entertaining football and though some critics said he had inherited a lot of good players when he had taken over after the war, they still had to be fashioned into a team and given the freedom to express themselves.

It was Manchester United's first Championship win for forty-one years and two trophies in his first five years as a manager established Busby as a manager of style and substance who would go on to become not only a legend but a legend in his own lifetime, with all manner of honours and tributes still to come.

Chapter Two

GENTLEMAN JOHN

═══════════

The most influential player in those early days was undoubtedly Johnny Carey, arguably the last of the great Corinthians in professional soccer, and he graced the Old Trafford club for seventeen years. Always known as 'Gentleman John', he had an easy-going, pipe-smoking demeanour, and was always calm and collected, even in later life when he was a manager.

He wasn't one of these Jekyll and Hyde characters who change once they get into sporting action. As John Doherty, who played with both the old guard and the Busby Babes, told me: 'I made my debut when John Carey was captain and I can't recollect him ever getting annoyed, not even if someone had kicked him. He seemed to stroll through games. If he were playing today he would be described as laid back; then we just thought he was unflappable.

'The big thing of course was that he was a great player and as captain his influence was immense. He was a thinker, not a shouter.'

Perhaps he didn't have to bellow and holler because he was

skipper of a great side made up mostly by mature men return-ing from the war who were disciplined with a sense of what needed to be done. They didn't have to be shouted at, and in that sense Johnny Carey was the right man, in the right place, at the right time.

He arrived at Old Trafford almost by accident, spotted by Louis Rocca, United's chief scout and a man who did a variety of other jobs for the club in an association that spanned an incredible fifty-five years.

Rocca tells the story of how he found Carey: 'I was sent over to Dublin to sign a player from Bohemians called Gaughan. Our manager at the time, Scott Duncan, told me that every-thing had been arranged for the lad to join us. My job was sim-ple – so it seemed – I just had to get him to sign the necessary forms and bring him back with me to Old Trafford.

'I contacted the player all right, only to learn of a snag. It appeared that Glasgow Celtic also wanted him and that as a Scottish club, they could pay any fee they liked. Gaughan nat-urally enough decided to hang on to see what would happen. He did in fact eventually sign for them and received a £400 fee. I spent the best part of a week trying to get him signed but on the Friday evening he became a Celtic player. Later he played for Southampton and Sunderland.

'I was upset by the whole thing but decided to stay over the weekend and on the Sunday went along to St James's Gate, then an unknown team to me. It was a poor game, but there was something about the inside right that took my fancy. I was satisfied he would make the grade, asked his name, and after the match went straight to the club secretary and told him of my mission.

'A meeting of the committee was called there and then. We

talked for hours and eventually I got Johnny Carey's signature for £200. Then I had to go to see Johnny's father – he was only seventeen at the time – but his consent was duly given and Mr Carey gave me a real homely Irish welcome that lasted into the early hours of the next morning.

'The next day young Johnny came to England with me. When we reached Manchester, he noticed a newspaper billboard that said: "United sign star". Johnny looked at me and we bought a paper. It told us that Ernie Thompson had signed for Manchester United from Blackburn. Then, right at the end, was a two-line paragraph about Johnny Carey's signing. Neither of us said anything!'

That was the embarrassing and inauspicious arrival in Manchester of the young Carey and it gave no indication of the distinguished service he would go on to deliver at Old Trafford for so many years.

For this was a youngster destined to become a giant among giants, a legend, a player who was so versatile that he figured in nine different positions for United, ten if you include the occasion he pulled on the goalkeeper's jersey after Jack Crompton had been taken ill at an away game.

Rocca later declared: 'No greater Irish player crossed the Channel to make a name in English football, and yes, I can recall stars like Billy Gillespie, Elisha Scott, Peter Doherty and Micky Hamill.'

Carey became Busby's onfield lieutenant, a captain who was the embodiment of his manager's philosophy. He led his team to honours, he was voted Footballer of the Year by the English soccer writers and he was fêted in the boardroom when he retired.

Naturally, he became an international, with the unusual

distinction of representing both the Republic of Ireland and Northern Ireland, and in 1947 he captained the Rest of Europe against Great Britain.

But all that was still to come. First he had to make his way at Old Trafford. Scott Duncan gave him his League debut early in 1937–38 in a home match against Southampton. United lost, but Carey held his place at inside right, only to end up on the losing side again when he next played. That was the end of his first run in the senior side. He got back in the first team just before Christmas, this time at inside left, and stayed to share in an unbeaten run that saw United finish runners-up in the Second Division.

The following year he made thirty-two appearances and scored six goals, helping United consolidate in the First Division, finishing a respectable fourteenth.

Then came the war and as a neutral from the Republic of Ireland, Carey could have gone back home, but he not only stayed, he enlisted to serve in the Queen's Royal Hussars.

'A country that gives me my living is worth fighting for,' he said with typical loyal sentiment. It was a gesture that proved a lengthy one as the war dragged on, yet I doubt he ever questioned his decision, because he was not that kind of man and his attitude was one of the things that endeared him to Manchester's sporting public.

Although a soldier, he continued to play in wartime football until he was posted to North Africa and Italy. He spent two years abroad after landing in Algiers and was then posted to Italy and stationed at Trieste. He played there for some of the local teams, who gave him an Italian feel by printing his name in the programme as 'Cario'. In the same unit was a young winger also destined for great things, Tom Finney.

Carey later told me: 'It was great fun. I had a job as a sergeant coaching and training all the football-minded personnel in the unit. It was good to get back to England, though, and link up with new players like Jack Crompton and Henry Cockburn'.

With players like Jack Rowley, Stan Pearson, Charlie Mitten and John Aston all returning from the Services, Busby was well off for forwards and he persuaded Carey to try fullback, softening any disappointment by making him the captain. Not that Carey would have objected (because nothing ruffled him) and he took to his new position like a duck to water. He played at fullback in the team that won the 1948 FA Cup and then in another shrewd Busby move he was switched to right half, where he became an even more majestic player in the 1952 Championship-winning team. He played thirty-eight League games that season and scored three goals in United's first League title since 1911.

In all, he made 306 League appearances, scoring 17 goals, and he would have totted up many more appearances had he not been robbed of six years by the war.

On the international front, the invitation to captain the Rest of Europe against Great Britain, to mark England's return to FIFA, came in May 1947 and a full-scale practice match was arranged for a friendly against Holland.

'I flew to Amsterdam to meet up with the other players. It was a strange experience with so many different languages being spoken. We didn't know each other, but we had a few good players and we beat the Dutch 2–1, which gave us high hopes of beating Great Britain,' he explained.

'We went to Scotland and stayed at the Marine Hotel in Troon to prepare for the match at Hampden Park. I shall always remember it because one of the waitresses complimented me on my command of English. I suppose I was a bit different from the other Europeans,' he added.

The game in Glasgow was watched by 140,000, and there was no holding the British team with players like Stanley Matthews, Wilf Mannion, Tommy Lawton, Billy Steel and Billy Liddell in their attack. They put six goals past Carey and the luckless French goalkeeper Daroi.

'It was no contest, really,' laughs Carey. 'Our team were like the strangers we were while the Great Britain boys knew exactly what they were doing. Still it was a great experience and a great honour to captain the Rest of Europe side.'

Carey won thirty-six caps for the Republic of Ireland, including a memorable 2–0 victory against England at Goodison Park in 1949 and was just as versatile on the international stage as he was for his club, appearing in seven different positions for his country, almost matching his ten for United.

Like Busby he had an aura of dignity that marked him out as someone special. His contribution to the 1952 Championship prompted a glowing tribute from the *Manchester Guardian* who accorded him and Busby the rare honour of a glowing mention in their esteemed leader column.

Their leader writer eulogised: 'After an interval of 41 years, Manchester United have regained the Championship of the Football League. The title has never been better earned.

'Not only has the team, in the five seasons before this one, finished second four times and fourth once in the League and won the FA Cup; it has been captained, managed and directed in a way that is a lesson to many others.

'J. Carey, the captain in this period, has been a model footballer – technically efficient thanks to hard work; a fighter to the last, without ever forgetting that he is a sportsman; a steadier of the younger and inexperienced, an inspirer of the older and tiring, and at all times the most modest of men, though he has won every football honour open to him.

'M. Busby, the manager, has shown himself as great a coach as he was a player, with an uncannily brilliant eye for young local players' possibilities, whether in their usual or other positions; a believer in the certainty of good football's eventual reward, and a kindly, yet, when necessary, firm father of his family of players.

'Between them they have built up a club spirit which is too rare in these days, a spirit which enables men to bear cheerfully personal and team disappointments and to ignore personal opportunities to shine for the good of the whole.

'Moreover, by eschewing the dangerous policy of going into the transfer market whenever a weakness develops and giving their chances instead to many local citizens on the club's books they have made it likely that this club will persist, since the club today is a Manchester one not in name only but in fact as far as most of its players are concerned.

'Manager and captain could never have brought about this happy state of affairs had they not had through these years such full authority and support from the board of directors as must be the envy of many other officials in all parts of the country.'

It was a very *Guardian*esque tribute but nonetheless well deserved, and United themselves knew they had been given exceptional service by their model player. When the moment came for his retirement in 1953, the directors took the unusual, perhaps unprecedented, step of inviting their captain to their boardroom.

The club minutes record: 'The directors expressed their deepest regret at his decision to end his playing career and unanimously agreed to put on record their great appreciation of his long and loyal service. By his outstanding personality as a true sportsman, the honours he had won as an international in club matches, he had covered his career with glory and set a shining example to all who follow him.'

The late Geoffrey Green, football correspondent of *The Times* in Carey's day, was another admirer and caught his character perfectly when he wrote in his official history of Manchester United: 'Here, indeed, was a man who had been one of the outstanding footballers of his time, an architect of constructive defence and almost as great in his way as Matthews the destroyer of defence. At first glance, with his thinning hair and thoughtful expression, he looked older than his true age. But there was no doubting his maturity. From the moment he led out his side, you got the impression that he was bringing out a pack of schoolboys who were to be put through their paces under his supervision.

'Not that he was overbearing. On the contrary. Yet there was something in his measured, stately tread that engendered an instant feeling of respect and authority. But Carey never encouraged any exploitation of his personality. For him the game was one thing; personal triumphs at best were an irrelevancy.

'Many other memories remain of Carey, the artist. His exact anticipation; the smooth unhurried positional play that carried him to the right place at the right moment with no more show than if he were taking a quiet stroll on a summer's evening; his exquisite balance and control, especially on a "sticky dog"; the way he measured his clearances, with the ball always used to the best advantage of the colleagues in front of him.

'And if sometimes he broke the accepted canons of a full-back by beating his opponent in the dribble near the danger zone, well, never mind, it was something that could be excused in him, because he was above the lesser mortals.

'For in effect he was a fullback who combined the constructive ability of wing half with the footwork and intelligence of an inside forward, and as such he mastered the arts and graces of the game. Carey, always the most generous of men and of opponents, had earned his plaudits to the end.'

When their captain decided to retire, United were keen to try to keep him on the staff. They knew that the qualities that had made him such a good player and influence were suited for management and the directors offered him a post as a coach. But Blackburn Rovers had also noted the potential and made him a better offer: as coach with the possibility of stepping up to become the manager.

Johnny opted for Blackburn and off he went to Ewood Park with the best wishes and appreciation of everyone at Old Trafford.

Matt Busby parted company with him somewhat reluctantly but told him he had all the necessary qualifications to become a full manager and urged him to try his luck.

The next phase of his career brought him mixed fortunes and turned out to be a tremendous challenge, at odds with his playing career which he had not only taken in his stride, but at something of a stroll. It had all come very easily to him, and things went well for him at Blackburn as he took them into the First Division. It was a success that caught the attention of Everton who offered him the manager's job at Goodison Park.

Carey said at the time: 'I've accepted the post of manager at Everton because it's a challenge I feel must be met. If I hadn't taken it, it's likely all the rest of my life I'd have wondered just how I would have gone on and how I'd have tackled the job of raising the team to its one-time greatness.'

Well, he found out the hard way, because just three years later he was the victim of one of the most bizarre sackings in football, and certainly one that shocked and disgusted his old mentor back at Old Trafford.

John Moores, the Everton chairman, sacked Carey in a London taxi as the two of them left a meeting of League clubs at the Café Royal where, ironically, the subject under discussion had been wages and contracts. He still had two and a half years of his contract to run but was given twenty-four hours' notice and had to go to court to get his contract paid up.

When he had arrived at Goodison, Everton were at the foot of the First Division table and in successive seasons he raised them to sixteenth and then fifteenth. When he was sacked they had been in a challenging second place and finished fifth, but chairman Moores had not liked a run of eight defeats and his eye had been caught by Harry Catterick, a former Everton player, doing well with Sheffield Wednesday.

Busby took exception to the cavalier treatment of his one-time captain, but Carey soon bounced back and after a short break became manager of Leyton Orient. He took them into the First Division, winning promotion as runners-up behind Liverpool, although they went straight back down again the following season.

His style of football remained creative and had echoes of the way he and his team-mates had played at Old Trafford. As he used to say: 'I just keep on telling them to play football, and play it on the ground, definitely no strong-arm stuff.'

One of the expressions he invariably used in his team talks to describe how he wanted his players to play was 'fizz it about'. It didn't sound very technical but you know what he had in mind, and his purist approach eventually found the right spiritual home with Nottingham Forest. For five years after becoming their manager in 1963 he enjoyed his best days in management, and they finished First Division runners-up in season 1966–67 behind Manchester United. Master and pupil were dominating the game and it's difficult to know who felt the proudest, Busby or Carey!

Carey had Tommy Cavanagh, later to become coach at Old Trafford under Tommy Docherty and Dave Sexton, as his assistant and together they made a good pair with 'Cav', a trainer who knew all about cracking the whip. But keeping Forest in the big-time proved difficult, and after half a season without a home win he was asked to leave. The wheel then completed a full circle when Blackburn Rovers appointed him as their administrative manager. He was back after a sixteen-year absence, but Rovers struggled, even after Carey swapped places with Eddie Quigley to take charge of the playing side, and they slipped down into the Third Division for the first time in their history.

That summer of 1971 proved the end of the management road for Johnny Carey and he settled into a quieter life away from football with a modest job in the Sale Treasurer's office, but he was never a man of pretension and as he said about his sacking: 'It's all part of the job.'

He went with head held high, too. He had never compromised his principles, nor his philosophy concerning the way the game should be played.

Tommy Docherty brought him back to the game when he

became manager of United as a part-time scout, but golf had become his main preoccupation by then. He was, in fact, a keen and able golfer at Bramhall Park in Cheshire and explained: 'Saturdays are given over to the golf now, but I still think football is a terrific game. I perhaps wish people would accept defeat with a little more grace and I would like to see the players allowed to express themselves more, but at the end of the day soccer is super, the best game in the world.'

You can just see Gentleman Johnny Carey taking a puff on his pipe as he delivers a verdict that sums up his philosophy of football and life.

Chapter Three

THE BOGOTÁ BANDIT

——

It takes all kinds to make a football team and on the left wing in Busby's post-war team was a man who contrasted startlingly with the gentlemanly image of Johnny Carey.

In fact they typecast Charlie Mitten as the bad boy of football and called him the 'Bogotá Bandit', but really, Charlie was simply a footballer ahead of his time.

His so-called crime was to believe that an individual had the right, just like the rest of us, to ply his trade as a professional footballer where he would be best rewarded.

The result was that when the Colombian club Santa Fe, who played in Bogotá, approached him with the offer of a £10,000 signing-on fee and wages of £60 a week, Charlie couldn't turn it down. It was a huge increase on the £8 a week (£6 in the summer) he earned for Manchester United and he always maintained: 'I had never seen that much money in my life before. If I had stayed with United for twenty-five years, I would never have made anything like it. I could have bought a row of houses with what the

Colombians were paying. It was an irresistible offer and I had to go.'

So off he went in the summer of 1950, following in the footsteps of Neil Franklin, the England and Stoke centre half. It seems hardly a sin, especially judged against the fortunes earned by some of today's well-travelled stars, but unfortunately Colombia were outside FIFA, so when he returned after a year, he was suspended, fined £250 and United placed him on the transfer list.

It meant United had him for only four seasons, though he certainly made his mark in those four years, making 142 League appearances and scoring 50 goals.

He was one of the great characters of the post-war era, and he turned left-wing play into an art form.

On his return to England, the self-styled 'Bogotá Bandit' was sold for £20,000 to Fulham and played there for five years before becoming player-manager at Mansfield Town. In 1958 he was appointed manager at Newcastle United where he indulged his passion for dog racing. It was said he had a hot line from his office at St James's Park to the local track and that he sometimes brought his favoured dogs into the ground for medical treatment.

He eventually returned to Manchester where he managed the White City dog track before turning to sports promotion, specialising in arranging tours abroad.

There was no doubt he made a big impact in Colombia because Real Madrid signed Santa Fe's two Argentinians, Alfredo di Stefano and Hector Rial, and were keen for Charlie to go to Madrid with them.

He could easily have become part of the Real Madrid side that dominated Europe at that time, winning the European

Cup for five successive seasons after its inception, but his wife, Bertha, preferred to come home. The need to educate his children also brought him back to be fined and banned.

In later years, Di Stefano, the maestro who so impressed United when they met Real Madrid in the European Cup in the fifties, was to tell him: 'Ah, Charlee Meeton, numero uno. If we have heem, we never need Gento. Gento, he queek, but Meeton, he more clever.'

As Charlie told me: 'Nice of him to say so, and it does make you wonder!'

There is no doubt Charlie's foreign adventure blighted his international career, as Sir Stanley Rous, secretary of the FA at the time, once told him: 'We know you are the best outside left in the country, but I'm afraid we can't select you for England because discipline must come first.'

Charlie's contemporaries describe his left foot as the 'sweetest' ever, and reckoned he could drop a centre on a sixpence. As for penalty taking, John Doherty, a former team-mate, remembers: 'United beat Aston Villa 7–0 at Old Trafford and Charlie Mitten scored three of his four goals with penalties.

'He hit the right-hand stanchion with his first and the left-hand one with his second. Then with the third he asked the goalkeeper which one he wanted this time. The keeper pointed and Charlie obliged with the goalkeeper still powerless to do anything about it.

'In my view there has never been a better outside left at Manchester United, as good as perhaps, but not better.'

Born in Rangoon (his father was in the Services), Charlie joined the club straight from school in 1936 and was ready for his senior debut when war broke out. He picked up his career again to help win the FA Cup in 1948 after serving in the RAF as a PT instructor and playing in wartime football. Then his sense of adventure took over and he was off. He never really forgave Manchester United for excluding him on his return. He expected to be fined but felt he should have been allowed to play for the Reds again.

But his disappointment did not prevent him from joining the Association of Former Manchester United Players. He was a regular at their functions and delighted in meeting up again with former team-mates. He even served as a Chairman of the Association and he never lost his love for United.

Charlie died in January 2002, a fortnight before his eighty-first birthday in a nursing home just outside Manchester in Styal. Former colleagues Jack Crompton and Johnny Morris were both at his funeral at Stockport Cemetery when his two boys, Charles and John, who both played for United in the six-ties, insisted that the service should be a celebration of their father's life rather than a day of mourning.

'That's what he would have wanted,' explained Charles jun-ior, and indeed, a smile and a quip were never far away when Charlie Mitten was around.

Manchester United have always had a soft spot for wingers and over the years some great performers have appeared on the flanks. Matt Busby certainly favoured width in his teams, so much so that despite having the penetration of Charlie Mitten at outside left, he made his first signing an outside right in order to give his forward line a thrust on the other flank too.

Hence the £4,000 purchase of Jimmy 'Brittlebones' Delaney from Glasgow Celtic, a pacey winger with a good scoring record of 79 goals in 178 League appearances for the Parkhead club. He helped Celtic to win two Scottish League

Championships and the Scottish Cup, but people thought Busby was taking a big gamble because the Scot had also suffered a terrible run of injuries, hence his nickname.

It turned out, though, that once installed in Busby's formidable front five he hardly missed a game.

He shared in the 1948 FA Cup win and had five good seasons, making a total of 164 League appearances as well as playing in 19 FA Cup-ties and scoring a total of 28 goals in the two competitions. He also won 13 Scottish caps.

He wanted to move back to Scotland in 1950 and Busby did not stand in his way with the result that he missed United's Championship success, but that was by no means the end of his career. He was thirty-six when he joined Aberdeen and finally shed his brittle-bones tag with another transfer, this time to Derry City in Northern Ireland where he won an Irish FA Cup medal to complete a unique hat trick of Cup successes in Scotland, England and Ireland.

He was close to picking up a Cup-winner's medal in a fourth country, too, when at the age of forty he was player-manager of Cork Athletic when they reached the final of the FA of Ireland Cup in the Republic. This time he was in the losing side, despite being two goals up against Shamrock Rovers at one point.

Delaney finally hung up his boots back home in Scotland with Highland League club Elgin City after twenty-three years as a player; not a bad playing record for someone with supposedly brittle bones.

Martin Edwards, when he was Chairman of United, was always intrigued by Delaney and in 1987 on a trip to Scotland went with Alex Ferguson to see him, as he was the only member of the 1948 FA Cup-winning team he had not met. Alex was pleased to make the introduction because in his own early playing days he had played with Jimmy's son Pat.

One of the results of the meeting was an invitation to Jimmy Delaney to be the guest of honour at a sportsmen's dinner at Old Trafford attended by most of his team-mates from the 1948 FA Cup-winning side. He had turned seventy but was fêted and thoroughly enjoyed a nostalgic return. He died two years later.

With Mitten on his overseas travels and Delaney back in Scotland, Busby had a wing problem but solved it by buying Johnny Berry from Birmingham City for the right flank and shuffling between Harry McShane and Ernie Bond on the left, until with a typical flash of genius, he moved Roger Byrne from left back to outside left. Byrne scored seven goals in the last six League games to clinch the Championship, while Berry made the right-wing berth his own for the next seven seasons.

Berry might not even have become a footballer had he not joined the Royal Artillery two years before the end of the Second World War. For it was while playing in unit football that he came to the attention of a fellow Gunner, Fred Harris, who also happened to be the captain of Birmingham City. The result was that just before the end of the war he was signed as a professional at St Andrews where he became a more than useful speedy right winger.

Busby signed him after recalling an impressive goal Berry had scored for Birmingham the previous season at Old Trafford and he happily paid £25,000 for his capture as he revealed: 'We signed Johnny Berry because every time we played Birmingham City he led us a merry dance.'

Berry was small but incredibly tough with a nickname of 'Digger' to reflect his willingness to get stuck in, and was one of only two players from the 1952 title-winning team to hold his place in the Busby Babes side that won the Championship in 1956 and 1957. In all he made nearly 300 League and Cup appearances for United, scoring 43 goals, until his career was cut short by the Munich crash.

He suffered severe head injuries in the 1958 accident and was never the same man again. He certainly had no chance of playing football again and my feeling now is that he should have received a lot more support than ever came his way.

After being looked after by Manchester United for a while he eventually left Manchester to return to his native Aldershot where he joined his brother Peter, a former Crystal Palace and Peterborough player, running a sports shop. He later worked in the warehouse of a television company, but there is no doubt that the crash wrecked not only his football career, but also his life. He died in 1968 aged sixty-eight, long before the memorial match featuring the return of Eric Cantona, to raise funds for the survivors and dependants.

Chapter Four

THE GUNNER

Although he figured on the wing at times early in his career, it was at centre forward that Jack Rowley took the eye, as he settled into Busby's first post-war team to become the legendary 'Gunner'.

The fans loved his cannonball shooting and his rocket headers; he was the archetypal barnstorming British centre forward. He wasn't called the Gunner for nothing, for he gunned his shooting with the kind of accuracy and ferocity he had used as an anti-tank gunner with the South Stafford infantry during the war. I have no idea how many tanks he hit as part of the invasion force in France during his six and a half years in the army, but he certainly made a habit of blasting the net as a footballer.

He scored 208 goals in 422 League and FA Cup appearances for United, an incredible record when you consider the war took more than six years out of his career, and he still managed to guest for other clubs when he was stationed in various parts of the country.

He has happy memories of his life as a solder-footballer as he once proudly told me: 'I played for Spurs one week and scored seven goals, and then a few days later I guested for Wolves and got eight of eight.'

Many consider he should have won more than six caps for England, but he played in the era of Tommy Lawton, Nat Lofthouse and Stan Mortensen. He still made his mark, though, scoring four goals in a 9–2 victory against Northern Ireland at Maine Road in 1949.

He dominated United's scoring in the post-war years, scoring twice in the FA Cup final victory over Blackpool in 1948 and setting a club League scoring record with thirty goals in the Championship season of 1951–52, a record that stood until Dennis Viollet raised the bar in 1959–60. That year he opened the season with hat tricks in the opening two games, and he was in fact the club's top scorer in each of the first four seasons after the war.

Jack was born in Wolverhampton into a footballing family. His father was a goalkeeper with Walsall, and was still playing for a local team at the age of sixty. His youngest brother, Arthur, was another phenomenon, who played for Leicester City and then created all manner of scoring records for Shrewsbury Town, including thirty-eight goals in the Third Division in the 1958–59 season.

When he left school he joined Major Frank Buckley's famous nursery at Wolverhampton Wanderers as a ground-staff boy. Playing as an outside left in those days, he was loaned out to Cradley Heath in the Birmingham League and transferred to Bournemouth.

Perhaps his face didn't fit in the disciplined academy run by Major Buckley, because Jack Rowley was an abrasive character and despite his prowess, not the most popular player in the dressing room.

There was nothing wrong with his ability, though, and after scoring ten goals in eleven League games at Bournemouth, Scott Duncan moved quickly to buy him for £3,000, a fee that turned out to be a bargain. He made his United debut against Sheffield Wednesday in October 1937, playing at outside left and sharing in a 1–0 win. He asked to play in the reserves to give himself time to adjust to his new club and when he was brought back into the first team after a month, he scored four goals in a 5–1 win against Swansea.

From then on, he never looked back and notched nine goals in twenty-five appearances, good going for an eighteen-year-old winger.

His goals were a key factor in United's promotion success and with ten in thirty-eight appearances the following year United were able to sign off for the war still a First Division club.

Back from the war, some six years later, he simply carried on where he had left off, rattling in even more goals. He started the first post-war season on the wing but soon found his way to centre forward and a tally of twenty-six League goals from thirty-seven appearances helped United to finish as League runners-up, just one point behind Liverpool.

Rowley and his goals were certainly decisive in the 1948 Cup run, especially his two equalisers in the final against Blackpool. Rowley remembered the first with relish, after Blackpool had taken an early lead, and afterwards said: 'The ball came through from Jimmy Delaney and caught goalkeeper Joe Robinson and Eric Hayward in two minds. They both called for it but I nipped between them as the keeper came for it and stuck out my foot. Luckily for me I connected. The ball went high in the air. I went round Robinson and then seemed to wait hours for the ball to come down. Eventually it did and I just had to side-foot it into the net.'

As one match report put it: 'It sounds easy, but only Jack Rowley would have been so nonchalant about it!'

Blackpool went ahead again, but once more Rowley came to the rescue with a goal to set up their 4–2 victory and bring the FA Cup back to Manchester United after an absence of thirty-nine years.

Rowley maintained his career average of a goal every two games, and particularly excelled in the Championship season when he contributed fourteen goals in the opening seven games. The team was getting a bit long in the tooth, though, and one by one they started to drop out. Rowley and Allenby Chilton played on for another three seasons until they, too, were squeezed out by the arrival of the brilliant Busby Babes. Jack lost his place to Tommy Taylor, and there was no disgrace in that, after a career with United that had spanned eighteen years. His last game for United was in January 1955, a 1–1 draw with Bolton Wanderers.

As you would expect he was granted a free transfer at the end of the season so that he could join Plymouth Argyle as player-manager. He played for two more years and then concentrated on the management side, and got Plymouth into the Second Division in 1959.

Football being the game it is, he was sacked six months later and it has to be said that his management style was a bit like his play on the field, aggressive and forthright, not always to everyone's taste, especially in those days when footballers were supposed to know their place and treat directors with respect.

Jack came back north to become manager of Oldham

Athletic and in three years he lifted the average attendance at Boundary Park from 4,000 to 15,000, as well as taking them up to the Third Division.

It still did not save him from the sack. At the very moment of their promotion triumph he was pushed out by a split board of directors and even Jack admitted: 'Some seem to think I'm too tough a boss. Well, I call a spade a spade and do some straight talking.'

Alas, it was too straight for a faction of the board, though not for the elderly chairman, Frank Armitage, who came out to say: 'It is disgusting that the manager of a club that has been lifted so high in the division should be sacked. This man has done wonderful things for this club. I am too disgusted for words.'

But the chairman had been outvoted and Jack Rowley was out of work, though not for long. The Gunner became one of the first English managers to be headhunted by a European club. Ajax had had experience of an English manager, however, and they signed Jack to take over from Vic Buckingham. He was immediately successful, taking the Amsterdam club to runner-up position in the Dutch First Division.

Unfortunately Jack ran into more politics – or possibly another personality clash – and his contract wasn't renewed.

He came home and was soon in demand, taking on managerial positions with Wrexham and Bradford. Then in 1968 came a second call from Oldham who wanted him to perform another miracle and keep them in the Third Division, where he had taken them in his previous time at Boundary Park. It was a move that suited him, because in his first spell in Oldham he had put down roots and taken over a Post Office and newsagent's shop in the nearby village of Shaw.

Jack welcomed the return with the words: 'I have some unfinished business at Boundary Park and I hate leaving loose ends. All the people involved in my previous time there have gone now and I don't have any bad feelings about that.'

This time, though, the magic didn't work. Oldham went down and at Christmas the following season they were knocked out of the FA Cup by a non-League team. They slid down the division until they were only two points above the bottom club. Inevitably the axe fell and that was the final curtain for Jack as a manager. It was a sad exit but he had plenty of happy memories and glory both as a player at Old Trafford and as a well-travelled manager.

'I enjoyed it all, playing and managing, but all good things come to an end,' he said, as he settled down in Shaw, surrounded by his family and becoming a regular visitor at his local Rugby Union club or as a guest at Swinton Rugby League club.

'I'm still interested in soccer, but it's convenient to watch the rugby three minutes' walk away. I also like the way they take the knocks, shake them off and then later are the best of pals in the bar. I was always hard but fair as a player and I see that kind of attitude more in rugby these days than I do in soccer,' he explained to me.

Jack died in June 1998, much mellowed of course, but he would be the first to admit that as a young man he did not suffer fools gladly and from time to time, he would clash even with Matt Busby, though Matt knew his value to the team and handled him with kid gloves.

Jack was certainly popular with the fans because they loved the brave and bustling style that brought him so many goals. He definitely had a fan in Bob Greaves, the television presenter and broadcaster, who was a familiar figure on Granada television for most of his working life and who idolised the Gunner, as well as the entire 1948 FA Cup-winning team. As he explained to me from his favoured watering hole, the Amblehurst Hotel in Sale: 'Heroes to a man, legends all, in an era when soccer pitches were seas of mud and the old leather ball seemed to weigh an old-fashioned ton.

'I was thirteen when they won the Cup, heard it on the wireless, saw the stilted highlights on the Pathé Newsreel at the pictures ... and I was hooked.

'My main hero was Jack (Gunner) Rowley. When I landed my first reporting job, aged sixteen, on the then *Sale and Stretford Guardian*, I would time my arrival at Cross Street en route to the office to catch a glimpse of him, tootling down the main road towards the ground, in his little Austin Standard, registration number HTU 924. I can't remember the number of my first car, but I've never forgotten his,' said the seventy-one-year-old one-time *Granada Tonight* reporter and BBC *Holiday* programme presenter.

'I didn't know Jack, you understand, and he certainly didn't know me ... that is, until a couple of years older, and certainly wilier, I persuaded my boss that I should do an interview with the Great Man, when he was chosen to go with an England squad to visit, if my memory is correct, Australia.

'I cycled on the office bike one evening by arrangement to the Rowleys' semi in Homelands Road, Sale (no mansions and security alarms in those long-ago days), met and chatted to Jack (bag of nerves I was) but not sufficiently nervy not to plan to leave my winter gloves at Chez Rowley, so I could go back a second time when Hero Man returned. Sad to relate, the best-laid schemes of mice and men and all that, only the charming Mrs R. was in when I next rang their doorbell.

'Hand on heart, I do believe I never met my hero again, but that doesn't mean I didn't see him away from the football field. In those days, myself and a group of mates used to cycle, yes cycle, to some away games, Liverpool and Everton in particular, and sometimes we'd catch a glimpse of our heroes when we caught up with their bus. Valhalla! Halcyon days!

'Another of my main men was the affable, courteous and gentlemanly John Carey, the captain. You can imagine my delight when I was fifteen or so, outside the ground at Old Trafford, when I managed to get his autograph. Not simply because I accomplished that, but because he looked down at me and said: "I've seen you before, Bobby, haven't I?"

'He knew my name because he had just written it as he signed his autograph. I probably blushed and blurted out that it just wasn't possible until he, the great Johnny Carey, remembered where and when.

'I had recently done a week in a professional play at the Hulme Playhouse in Manchester (only a cameo part) and he had been in the audience one night, it turned out, and HE recognised ME.

'I didn't come down for a month!

'And then, just a few years ago, when I mentioned this episode in a newspaper column, his wife wrote to me at Granada, telling me Johnny wasn't at all well, and asking me to send him MY autograph.

'Sadly, he, Jack, Charlie Mitten and one or two more from that great team have gone to the great stadium in the sky but I will never forget them. I once wagged off school in the fifties and saw Charlie, the Cheeky Chappie, score three penalties against Aston Villa at Old Trafford. I forget the details but what I do know for sure is that before each penalty Charlie pointed to exactly where he intended to send his shot, and three times he was inch perfect and the goalie knew nothing about them.

'Now that's the way I like my legends, and that's the way I like to remember them.'

Chapter Five

A LOVELY MAN

The dressing room were all agreed, not only was Stan Pearson a brilliant player, he was also a lovely man with it!

Matt Busby always described him as the brains of his talented forward line, and indeed, he had so many qualities, with the possible exception, some say, that he was just a tad too nice.

Certainly, there wasn't such a thing as a nasty streak in his make-up, though personally I doubt whether a more cynical approach to the game would have made any difference, because he simply had so much skill that he didn't have to put himself about.

Stan had everything and was the classic, old-fashioned inside forward. He was creative, subtle, enjoyed employing a deceptive body swerve, had tremendous skill on the ball and could pass it like a dream; then on top of all that, he was an outstanding goal scorer.

He formed the other half of a dream striking partnership with Jack Rowley; they complemented each other perfectly. Pearson created many of Rowley's goals with his intuitive scheming and profited from the big man's more forceful approach.

He made 345 League and FA Cup appearances, scoring 149 goals, a great scoring rate, and as with Rowley, achieved these figures despite losing over six years to the Second World War. As Busby's first team gathered momentum in the coming years, he scored a semi-final hat trick against Derby to send United to Wembley in 1948. He said afterwards: 'All the time I was thinking of Matt Busby's words when he said that the greatest thrill in soccer is playing at Wembley on Cup final day, and that I'm now going there!' In the final he scored the goal that put United in front for the first time in the match on their way to a 4–2 victory.

Four years later he contributed twenty-two goals to help win the League Championship. His scoring partnership with Rowley was just too good for the rest of the First Division.

He used to say about the team that gave their young manager his first trophies: 'For two or three seasons our forward line picked itself. We all got to know each other so well that instinctively we knew what was going to happen next. For instance if John Aston had the ball at left back I would come towards him, and I knew without looking that if I slipped it straight, Jack Rowley would be moving for it. He would then push it out to Charlie Mitten on the left wing and within seconds we had the ball in front of goal. I always knew without looking where Jack Rowley would be running.

'They talk about one-touch football these days as if it is something new, but we were doing it just after the war and in my opinion, no team has done it better,' he added.

As a boy Stan Pearson played for Salford Schools and joined United aged fifteen in 1936. He made his debut at the age of seventeen in a 7–1 win at Chesterfield, and he scored in each of the next two games to win a regular place, but he only had two seasons before war interrupted normal football.

He served in the South Lancashire Regiment in India where he played in a British Army touring football team with players like Arsenal's Denis Compton, to entertain the troops. Also out touring and playing football in India at that time was Johnny Morris, another of the soldier-footballers who were to come together after the war to such telling effect, in the first team Busby built.

During the war he also guested for Newcastle, Brighton and Queens Park Rangers.

Stan went on to complete seventeen years of service with Manchester United, and ironically it was his loyalty to Old Trafford that finally brought the curtain down on his United playing days.

He explained to me: 'I remember Jimmy Murphy asking me to come with him to Maine Road to talk to a youngster he was trying to sign for Manchester United. There was a problem in so much as all his family were City fans and wanted him to go to the Maine Road club. He was an inside forward like me so Jimmy thought that I might be able to help win him over to a career at United. I had a good chat with the boy and did my best to persuade him that Old Trafford was the place to be. I must have done quite a good job because he did in fact sign for United ... and it was not long before Dennis Viollet took my place in the team!'

Stan moved to Bury in 1954 and he later played for Chester before becoming the manager. When that came to grief, he settled at Prestbury in Cheshire where he ran the local Post Office and newsagent's with the same kind of diligence and thoroughness that always accompanied his football.

'I used to get up at 5.30 a.m. to do the morning papers and I enjoyed it. I hated the thought of doing nothing and over the years I was a regular spectator at Old Trafford.

'I was first taken to see United when I was seven in 1926. I remember being impressed by a right half with a bald head called Frank Mann, and from then on I was a United fan,' he said.

Stan still made time to coach his local Prestbury amateur team and he continued to live in the village until his death in February 1997.

The final member of the Fabulous Five up front for Busby was, of course, Johnny Morris, the baby of the side and a feisty character whose departure from United – under something of a cloud – meant that he never enjoyed the status of the rest of the forward line.

Not that that would worry the bright, you might say cocky, Morris, who always has a smile and a quip when you meet him at one of the functions for United old boys or on a golf day. In fact, he thrived on the golf course in later life and was always a keen competitor at the Association's golf competitions, once winning despite being the oldest man on the course.

His arrival at Old Trafford was orthodox enough. He hailed from Radcliffe near Bolton and was spotted for the Manchester United Junior Athletic Club (MUJAC) youth scheme. He signed forms for the club in 1941 and played on loan at Bolton for a spell. The war caught up with him, as it did for most of the fit young men in those perilous times, and so off he went as a trooper in a tank regiment of the Royal Armoured Corps. When he got back home Busby had no hesitation in making him part of his all-star attack and many good judges reckoned he was the complete inside forward. He was so good that he established partnerships all over the field. He loved to pick out Charlie Mitten from deep inside right to outside left; he had a good understanding with Jimmy Delaney in front of him. He could link up with his fellow inside forward, Stan Pearson, and he was a great source of ammunition for the Gunner at centre forward. He could also score goals himself.

He played a big part in establishing United as a major force after the war, and delivered a particularly good performance in the 1948 Cup final. But after only three seasons came the bust-up with Busby and a transfer to Derby County, for a then record fee of £24,500.

What was it all about?

Well, there was general unrest in the dressing room because the players felt they deserved more than just a medal for packing Wembley and thrilling everyone with their Cup final performance and Johnny Morris was just the man to put the complaints into words. He was afraid of no one, on or off the field, and he could argue a good case. The rebellion was squashed but trouble erupted again at the start of the Cup competition the following year.

Johnny's argumentative style was giving the manager headaches and this time Busby didn't hesitate. Even though Morris was one of his best players, he moved him out. It was a typical and classic instance of a manager establishing his authority and making it clear that no one player was bigger than either the club or, for that matter, the manager.

Jack Crompton, the goalkeeper at the time and later the trainer, reckons it was the moment when Busby indicated that he was going to be a major figure as a manager.

He told me: 'Naturally, when Matt Busby first took charge he had to fight to make his presence felt and he had still to win the great respect he enjoyed later. I think he had the sympathy of the players as someone fresh from our ranks, in his first job as a manager and I am sure he would have agreed that the players were patient and understanding. But, of course, a manager must command more than that from his players and though his outstanding ability was apparent after only a few months, I think he was still feeling his way, up to the 1948 Cup final win. Ironically, it was his first major trophy success, evidence to all and sundry that he was a man destined to do big things in football, that brought the one and only crisis between players and club that I can remember.

'We went on strike a few months after the final for something we thought we should have. Details don't matter now and I only mention the incident to show that he did not win his place as a master manager without his share of problems. It was finally sorted out, though it took a little while before the trouble was forgotten. It was a big test for a comparatively new boss and it was probably only due to his ability as a manager of men that the problem was finally compromised.

'No doubt he had many a struggle to get his way at board meetings, though as a player I could feel his presence becoming more widely felt all the time. I realised that he had really won his battle when another challenging problem arose in 1949, as we were heading for the Cup final again.

'Johnny Morris, our talented inside forward, was giving the Boss some headaches and after dropping him for one Cup tie, he had him transferred to Derby. To my mind, if Johnny had stayed we would have reached the final again. (United were knocked out 1–0 in a semi-final replay at Goodison Park, by

Wolves, after a 1–1 draw at Hillsborough.)

'Naturally the players thought the club should have kept him. I thought so, too, at the time, but this is where you live and learn and time proved that the manager was right to stick to his beliefs. Johnny Morris was transferred on a matter of principle. Matt must have had a tremendous fight with his own conscience and with other people before taking such a drastic step. I can appreciate now that he was right and it is this almost uncanny foresight and judgement, even if it involved an unpopular decision, that kept Manchester United at the front in post-war football.'

Johnny had three years at Derby and during this spell he won three England caps. His contemporaries think it should have been more. He moved on to Leicester City and twice helped them to the Second Division Championship.

He became player-manager at Corby Town and did a similar job at Kettering Town, before managing Rugby Town, Great Harwood and Oswestry Town. He left football in 1969 and worked as a tyre salesman back in Cheshire until his retirement, when golf became the light of his sporting life. But he will always be remembered as the perky, outspoken character who had given Matt Busby problems all those years ago.

Chapter Six

A DREAM TEAM

═══

Behind every great man stands not just a good woman but, at least in terms of football, a good water carrier, as Eric Cantona famously described the players who make up the rest of the team.

That was the beauty of Matt Busby's dream team after the war. Every United fan, at least of a certain age, can rattle off the bewitching forward line of Delaney, Pearson, Rowley, Morris and Mitten, because they were the galacticos of their day. Not so many can go through the rest of the side.

But they, the water carriers, were an essential element of the success of Busby's first trophy-winning team: men like John Aston, who deserved to be regarded as a galactico himself, after winning seventeen England caps at left back, in the very competitive era that followed the war. Indeed, he was an outstanding club servant, who stayed on after his playing career to become a junior coach and later the chief scout, in an Old Trafford career spanning thirty-five years.

As a schoolboy and junior he played on the old United grounds of Newton Heath and Bank Street in Clayton before signing for United as an amateur in 1937. He didn't have time to make a senior mark before the war took him away as a Royal Marine and Commando for the duration. He became a professional after he was demobbed and it didn't take him long to establish himself in the first team. He played in Busby's opening line-up, in season 1945–46, was a member of the FA Cup-winning team of 1948 and the only ever-present in United's League and Cup campaign that season. He was also part of the 1952 Championship team and figured just as regularly for England in that period.

Although left back became his regular position, he was a good all-round footballer who actually joined United as an inside forward. Busby came up with the inspired decision to move him to fullback, but did not hesitate in switching him to up front again, to replace the injured Jack Rowley midway through the 1950–51 season. He was so successful at centre forward that he scored fifteen goals in twenty-two games and forced the returning Rowley out on to the left wing.

It was good for Manchester United, but not so clever for Aston's international career with Walter Winterbottom insisting that he would only select a current left back for England. Even though John returned eventually to left back for United, he never played for England again, not that he ever complained, he wasn't that kind of man.

He made his last appearance in 1954, his career end hastened by tuberculosis, along with the emergence of the Busby Babes. He moved into a coaching position and then scouting. He was chief scout under Frank O'Farrell and suffered in the fall out when O'Farrell and Malcolm Musgrove were sacked in 1972. His departure was bitter, understandably so, after such lengthy and varied service. He asked chairman Louis

Edwards for the reasons behind his sacking and was told that the club were not satisfied with his scouting activities. The suggestion was resented at the time and never really forgiven, which is sad because older supporters will remember with great affection his peerless play in those heady post-war days.

After leaving Old Trafford he worked for Freddie Goodwin, the former United player and cricketer who had become manager at Birmingham City. He became chief scout at St Andrews, but again failed to survive a club upheaval when Alf Ramsey took over.

By that time he had little heart left for football and he concentrated, with his brother, on the family business. He eventually returned to the Old Trafford fold by supporting the functions organised by the Association of Former Manchester United Players, until illness prevented him from doing so.

Nobody can take away his service to Manchester United, though, service that was continued when his son, John Aston junior, joined the club to create a unique family achievement.

There have been a number of famous father and son partnerships playing for the same team, not least Alec and David Herd who played in the same Stockport County side. To the best of my knowledge, though, I don't think any father and son have won Championship medals for the same club ... big John in 1952, of course, and young John in 1967.

Both men were immensely proud of the family association which even had a parallel on the Cup front, dad winning the FA Cup in 1948 and his son twenty years later collecting a European Cup winner's medal, and as young John was always delighted to point out: 'Red is United's colour, but we both won our Cup medals playing in royal blue shirts.'

Another self-effacing player who went on to contribute hugely to United's backroom staff was goalkeeper Jack Crompton. Jack was Mr Reliable as a goalkeeper, indeed as a person. Born in Hulme, Manchester, he arrived at Old Trafford just before the end of the war through the local works side, Goslings, a team used by United as something of a nursery. He was in Busby's opening team, and as his team-mates will say in later chapters, he was a key figure in the FA Cup success in 1948. His highlight was not just stopping, but catching a pile-driver from Stan Mortensen when the score was level at 2–2 and then making the long quick clearance that caught Blackpool on the hop – allowing Stan Pearson to streak away and put United in front.

He was a fitness fanatic, a great supporter of the YMCA, a keen walker and he was still playing tennis in his sixties. Long after he had finished with the professional game, he could be found working in the evenings coaching young people on the all-weather pitches at Manchester City's Platt Lane training complex. He even had a stab with the Brooklands hockey team after I had taken them there for a dose of the Crompton treatment, though we didn't let him loose with a hockey stick after seeing what he thought it could be used for!

He made 212 League appearances for United but only played a handful of games in the Championship season, before losing his place to Reg Allen, an £11,000 signing from Queens Park Rangers. Busby also signed a young goalkeeper, Ray Wood, from Darlington and eventually Jack found himself providing reserve cover for the rapidly developing younger man.

He left Old Trafford in 1956 to become trainer at Luton Town with the long-term plan to return to United in some similar capacity after he had gained experience on the management side. Events dictated an earlier return than he had intended, with the Munich air crash leaving United desperately short of training staff following the deaths of Tom Curry and Bert Whalley. It was an emergency, but as you might imagine from such a genuine character as Jack Crompton, he answered the SOS immediately to become the United trainer, first working with Jimmy Murphy and then, of course, with Matt Busby once the manager had recovered from his injuries.

He shared in all the momentous successes of the sixties, in the days of Bobby Charlton, Denis Law and George Best, always working to keep feet on the ground in those exciting times.

He left in 1971 soon after Matt Busby had stepped down as manager. He stayed on long enough to ease Wilf McGuinness into management, but I'm sure he sensed that it was the end of an era, which indeed it was, and he left to manage Barrow before coaching at Bury and then for Bobby Charlton at Preston North End. He returned to Old Trafford in 1974 to spend seven years looking after the reserve team, even briefly becoming caretaker manager in charge of a summer tour to the Far East in 1981.

Then, he bowed out. Matt Busby never had a more loyal clubman, who never wavered in his support for the man he called the Boss, nor in his admiration for the man he worked for as both player and trainer. He told me: 'As a manager, Matt Busby never lost the common touch, the knack of understanding, and being in touch with players. He never forgot a player, past or present, and his memory for people's names was uncanny. He was so thoughtful, too. I remember our first flight to the Continent after the Munich disaster. After we landed at Amsterdam Airport, Bill Foulkes telephoned his wife to let her know we had arrived safely. Teresa Foulkes already knew.

Busby had already been on the phone to tell her, so concerned was he in the aftermath of Munich and the fact that her husband had been in the crash.'

Goslings supplied another of the players for Busby's initial team, appearing in both the Cup and Championship teams. The late Henry Cockburn was your typical little guy, making up for a lack of height with fire and fury. He was a bubbly character, too, with a reputation as someone who never stopped talking, though that didn't stop him flying into tackles, outjumping taller opponents and generally covering every blade of grass on the pitch. He had the kind of abrasive qualities that later also made Nobby Stiles such an effective player, and like Nobby, he was popular with his team-mates who admired his ability as a right-footed player who excelled at left half. He worked well with Johnny Aston behind him and Charlie Mitten in front and nobody begrudged him his thirteen caps and his place in a talented international halfback line with Billy Wright and Neil Franklin.

He was given his first cap after only seven First Division appearances, such was the impact he made after joining United from Goslings during the war in 1943.

He played for nearly ten years at United, making 275 appearances before being squeezed out by the arrival of Duncan Edwards. Too passionate about his football to settle for the reserve side – and he was well aware that Edwards, once in the side, would not be going back to the second string – he moved on to Bury and then Peterborough. He didn't mind going non-League, such was his wish to keep playing for as long as possible, and he finished his playing career in his late thirties with Corby Town and Sankeys of Wellington, in the West Midlands Regional League. He returned to the Football

League as trainer and coach at Oldham Athletic and Huddersfield Town.

When he was at Peterborough he worked part-time for the local newspaper and one of the tasks that fell to him was to write the bills announcing the Munich air crash, including the bulletins of Duncan Edwards' fight for life.

But if Henry was tough, he was as nothing compared with the man beside him at centre half, and he was big with it, too. Nobody argued with Allenby Chilton. He was a hard man and fitted, exactly, into the mould that Matt Busby liked in the middle of his defence, starting with Chilton and finishing with Bill Foulkes. The idea was to command the middle of your own half and then give the ball to those around who could produce something creative.

He fitted the bill exactly and as a man who had originally trained to become a boxer, he was not easily moved. He started his football life at Liverpool but couldn't make the breakthrough at senior level, so he moved down the East Lancashire Road and enjoyed a debut on the day before war was declared. Originally from the North East, he joined the Durham Light Infantry and it was another seven years before he was able to pick up his football career again. He was wounded twice, once at Caen and then again in the Normandy D-Day landings.

Busby hadn't forgotten him though and on his return he went straight back into the team and stayed there for the next ten years. He lasted longer than most of his wartime comrades and in fact had just completed a club record of 166 successive games when Mark Jones finally edged him out.

He had served Busby well, no frills and perhaps not the easiest man to manage, but he was a cornerstone of the team that launched Busby into successful management.

The juniors certainly didn't give him any cheek, as former Busby Babe John Doherty recalls in his excellent book, the *Insider's Guide to Manchester United*: 'As a youngster I was unfortunate to find myself with him one night in Scarborough, where we had gone for a week's special training in the middle of winter. We stayed at the Grand Hotel and the lads were going out in the evening, but Allenby ordered me to stay with him. It turned out that my job was to go and fetch his drinks from the bar, and to pay for them! But that was Big Chilly and somehow, strange as it may seem now, I never resented him for it and always felt a certain warmth towards him. You have to bear in mind that men like him had fought in a war. They had done things and faced things that we never had to, which set them apart.'

Certainly another of the legends! Indeed, there were so many characters around in this era that it is difficult to know where to stop. John Anderson, one of the Cup final stars on the other side of Chilton, was only on the scene for a year, but he made his mark. So, too, did Harry McShane, signed from Bolton to replace the rebel Charlie Mitten. Injury robbed him of a Championship medal, just two appearances short of qualifying, but he was another who found it difficult to walk away permanently from Old Trafford. He left to play for Oldham, but later linked up with the Reds to become the club's first announcer and presenter, working over the public address system, and then he scouted for the club for twenty years.

I mustn't forget Johnny Downie either, signed from Bradford Park Avenue for £18,000 to replace Johnny Morris. They reckoned he was brilliant in training but lost some of his confidence on the big stage. Nevertheless he chipped in with eleven goals to help win the 1952 League title and made over a hundred League appearances before moving to Luton.

Even Manchester United's water carriers in this golden age could play a bit.

Chapter Seven

GRAND OLD MEN

S adly, the march of time means that the grand old men who played in Matt Busby's original team after the war are one by one gradually slipping away from us. In fact only Jack Crompton, John Anderson and Johnny Morris are left now from the team that won the FA Cup in 1948.

So I'm pleased that when I was editing the *LEGENDS* magazine for the Former Manchester United Players Association I took the opportunity in February 2000, along with writer Ivan Ponting, of inviting the team survivors to Old Trafford to reminisce about playing for such a crack side.

Charlie Mitten was still around and he joined Jack Crompton, John Anderson and Johnny Morris along with Ivan and me for a walk down memory lane. As Ivan imaginatively put it at the time: 'They might have still been dancing across the turf in their own theatre of dreams ... Goalkeeper Jack Crompton gathering the ball safely and throwing it to the feet of wing half John Anderson who, in his customary constructive manner, dispatches a probing pass to Charlie Mitten on the left flank. The finest of all uncapped English wingers accelerates past one hapless opponent, then feints beguilingly to leave another for dead, before crossing with unerring accuracy towards the dark curls of Johnny Morris. The fearless little schemer drifts between two hulking defenders, times his leap to perfection and his precise header arrives crisply at its only conceivable destination, the corner of the opposition's net!'

The incomparable class of 1948 are back in harness, and it's like they've never been apart. Of course, a modicum of dramatic licence has been taken here. All four men are in their seventies now and their most recent sporting exploits are of the golfing rather than footballing variety.

But the spirit and comradeship which suffused Sir Matt Busby's first magnificent Manchester United side remains as potent as ever. Thus, when this sprightly, articulate quartet assembled for a natter in the grill room at Old Trafford, the years seemed to roll back as smoothly as a through-ball from the cultured boot of their old team-mate, the late and much-lamented Stan Pearson.

There was Johnny Morris, the 'baby' of the team, feisty, irrepressible and looking more like a man in his late fifties than a septuagenarian; Charlie, the 'Bogotá Bandit', eyes still twinkling and with his cutting wit unimpaired; Jack, quietly courteous, oozing dignity and brimming with wisdom; and John Anderson, sprightly, affable and with total recall of the momentous events which enchanted the sporting world more than half a century ago.

Unavoidably absent through a prior engagement was wing half Henry Cockburn, still living in Ashton-under-Lyne, while John Aston, the left back, was missing, stricken by a long-term illness. Both have died since our meeting, along with Charlie

Mitten and the other five FA Cup winners of 1948, skipper and right back John Carey, centre half Allenby Chilton, right winger Jimmy Delaney, spearhead Jack Rowley and inside forward Stan Pearson. All have passed away, though their names cropped up constantly. They will never be forgotten, not just because they were wonderful footballers, but because the team spirit of the 1948 combination was, and remains, second to none.

That much was evident by the sharpness and underlying affection of the banter which got under way even before the old comrades took their places at the table. Predictably enough, first into their stride were that irreverent duo, Messrs Morris and Mitten.

With Johnny's controversial 1949 move to Derby County under discussion, someone asked whether the future Sir Matt, so famously avuncular, could be unforgiving when crossed.

Said Johnny: 'We had a disagreement over my benefit payment, but I didn't blame him personally. I would do the same if I was a manager and it happened to me.'

Charlie: 'I'm not so sure. If I'd been in charge, I would have looked at the quality of the player involved.'

Johnny: 'Quality of the player? Are you telling me I was no blooming good?'

Charlie: 'You catch on quickly, John!'

'And to think, all these years I thought you were my mate,' came the reply.

They dissolved into laughter, clearly thinking the world of each other, both as men and as footballers.

Then, with today's exorbitant wages under the microscope, Jack remarked on the intense enjoyment the 1948 team extracted from life, adding dryly: 'At least the lads of today can be miserable in comfort.' Johnny Anderson agreed that while the old-timers were anything but handsomely remunerated, they enjoyed the game more than the heroes of the late 1990s did: 'We loved every minute of it. Most of us would have played for nothing,' he said.

Jack Crompton's considered assessment was typically thoughtful: 'A major factor in our success was the discipline in the side. Most of the players came from the forces and the camaraderie of wartime made us close. When peace came, we appreciated the freedom and being paid for playing the game we loved. We were such a close-knit bunch that any one of us could have spoken for the other ten and that despite the usual mix of personalities you would find anywhere. We had our extroverts like Johnny Morris and jokers like Charlie, who was always quick-witted and light-hearted, while a lot of us were quieter. John Carey, the skipper, was a diplomat with a touch of the blarney, while Allenby Chilton was our leader on the field, a screamer and a shouter, but always one of the lads.

'At one of the Former Players' earliest dinners, I remember that the artist Harold Riley said to me: "The nicest thing about seeing you all is that you seem to be so genuinely pleased to be reunited." And that was right. We were a team on and off the pitch. There were no prima donnas. We were all broke together, all on the bus together, all on a level. It was a different world.'

In view of such solidarity, why did three of the assembled company – the two Johnnies and Charlie – leave Manchester United while they still had plenty to offer on the field? The answer came back quite clear and simply: 'Money!'

None of them held a grudge, but there is little doubt that they would all have enjoyed longer careers at Old Trafford if the Red Devils' purse strings had not been quite so tightly drawn.

Explained Johnny Anderson: 'I thought I was entitled to a benefit, but the board didn't, so it was time to move on. In fairness, there was also the fact that Matt liked to change and freshen his side after he had won something. United had some great youngsters coming through, including Duncan Edwards, who was obviously an exceptional talent.' The result was that John Anderson joined Nottingham Forest in October 1949 and received the all-important gratuity that, by the regulations pertaining then, was his due following the move.

The plan to make some money hatched by Johnny Morris, bearing in mind that he was an important spoke in the team wheel, was cunning to say the least. He explained: 'I kept asking for a benefit, which I felt was owed to me, but I got nowhere. So I wanted a transfer but Matt Busby told me: "While I am here you will never leave the club." But I had heard whispers that there might be interest from both Derby and Liverpool and I wasn't going to give up that easily.

'Now around that time we had a golf tournament for players and staff and I won it. I've still got the medal. That reminded everyone that I wasn't a bad golfer so I thought I might turn it to my advantage. I went to see the secretary, Walter Crickmer, and demanded my cards. I told him I was packing in football to become a golf professional. He couldn't believe his ears at first, but in the end, United fell for it. They knew that if they sold me to Derby they would get a decent fee, but that if I turned to golf they would get nothing.'

Thus a deal was struck: with United pocketing £24,500, Johnny moved to the Baseball Ground, where he replaced the great Raich Carter and went on to win three England caps.

'I didn't regret what I did for a moment. I had to do it to better myself and for the good of my family. The only aspect that bothered me was leaving my team-mates, who were the best bunch imaginable. We were a brilliant side, but I would never have made any money if I'd stayed at United. I would have won a lot more medals perhaps, but you can't live on medals!'

Jack Crompton was in no doubt about that last point: 'If Johnny had stayed we would have won the FA Cup for a second and maybe a third time. I think we'd have won the Championship sooner too.'

As it was, the Red Devils finished runners-up in 1946–47, 1947–48, 1948–49 and 1950–51, before finally claiming the elusive crown the following season. But the departure of Charlie Mitten to continue the break-up of Busby's first great side was the most sensational exit of all. It was 1950 and despite English clubs making massive profits during the post-war football boom, a top professional could expect to earn merely £8 per week in the winter and £6 in the summer. Against that background, and frequent muttering about a strike by understandably discontented players, Charlie was offered the lucrative contract described earlier to join the Colombian club, Santa Fe of Bogotá.

As he says: 'It was an irresistible offer and I had to go.'

But Charlie was monstrously unlucky. At the time he walked out on United, Colombia were outside FIFA and anyone playing there was considered a footballing outlaw. But after one season in the sun for the Mitten family, the South American nation was readmitted to the sport's governing body on condition that the 'rebels' were sent home.

'The timing couldn't have been worse for me. I was greeted as if I was a criminal and frozen out by people whom I had counted as friends. Matt Busby was a great manager, and I know his hands were tied to a large extent, but after all we had been through together, I think he might have done a bit more for me. As it was, I was suspended for six months and fined £250, after which I joined Fulham, where I had some enjoyable years.'

Just to emphasise Charlie's bad luck, during his time in Bogotá, Real Madrid attempted to sign the cream of the Colombian mercenaries. They took the two fabulous Argentinians, Alfredo di Stefano and Hector Rial, and they were desperately keen to take Mitten, too, but his wife was homesick and felt their children needed an English education, so Charlie never went to Spain.

But, looking back, none of the four grand old men of Manchester United gathered round that dining table were in the business of bitterness. There, in the heart of a modern foot-balling empire, whose spiritual foundations they had helped to lay, they talked with pleasure, wit and humility, but no false modesty, of noble deeds and a simple sporting life which has vanished for ever.

Sure, there were financial injustices a long time ago, but they knew in their hearts that the team they graced will go down as one of the finest ever. And deep down, to men like this, that's enough.

Chapter Eight

THE FAB FIVE

I t was the team that pioneered the modern tradition of Manchester United, always daring to attack, so that it might entertain and win, but never afraid to risk gallant defeat. In terms of soul, if not of accumulated silverware, it touched genuine greatness.

Gloriously, despite finishing second in a series of title races, Matt Busby's first lovely fusion of artistry, verve and resilience did have its day, putting to the sword a fine Blackpool side which starred the two illustrious Stans, Matthews and Mortensen in the FA Cup final of 1948. For sustained, free-flowing skill and high adventure, that gala performance by the blue-shirted Red Devils has never been matched in a major final and, given the stranglehold of today's safety-first tactics, it is safe to say we shall not see its like again.

The names of the eleven heroes are enshrined for ever in Old Trafford folklore but, for the uninitiated or the very young, they bear repetition.

Between the posts was Jack Crompton, the very antithesis of flamboyance but reassuringly reliable and a magnificent athlete. As Johnny Morris recalls: 'Matt Busby used to say that there might be some argument about who was the best goalkeeper in the country, but there was none about who was the fittest.

'Crompo would train most of the day with the lads before popping round to the YMCA for a bit more work, then head up into the mountains for an evening stroll. He never let us down. We played on some poor pitches and with a bumpy old ball, but Crompo didn't make silly mistakes.'

Johnny Anderson had a specific memory of Jack's athleticism and awareness, as recalled here: 'The turning point of the '48 final was when the score was 2–2 with not long left and Morty (England centre forward Stan Mortensen) was through on goal. He shot hard but Jack reached it and should by rights have tipped it away, but somehow he caught it and threw it out to me. I looked up and saw that both Stan Pearson and Johnny Morris were free ahead of me. I chose Stan and, seemingly all in one movement, he gathered the ball, turned and scored.

'It was a great goal, but it wouldn't have been scored without Jack.'

At right back was the side's figurehead, John Carey, an archetypal soft-brogued Dubliner and a thoroughbred allround footballer. Johnny Morris grins: 'They called him Gentleman John, and that was appropriate provided he got the ball! He was a lovely lad, perhaps too nice at times to be the skipper, but there was always Allenby Chilton to give us a gee-up.'

Carey lived with the Mitten family for a time after crossing the Irish Sea as a youngster, and Charlie remembers: 'He was a terrible inside left in the A team when he started, but he became a brilliant fullback. He was a good ball-player, as we all had to be.' John was renowned for his coolness, but Morris stresses that the captain knew how to enjoy himself. 'Travelling home from games he was always in charge of the sing-songs on the bus. He livened up plenty after a game,' he said.

The left back was John Aston, another skilful individual though slightly quicker than his partner. Johnny Morris again: 'He was versatile and he went on to play at centre forward for a while after I had left United. He was so good with the ball that it was like having an inside forward at fullback.'

Jack Crompton describes Aston as a lively, bouncy fellow, utterly straight and an immense asset to the team. After retirement as a player, he rendered further service to the club as coach and chief scout.

Johnny Anderson played at right half, bringing both creativity and determination to his work, and he remembers vividly his moment of Wembley glory, when he scored the match-clinching final goal.

'John Aston had the ball and I was running forward, because we didn't like to go backwards in our day. After all, we had five fantastic forwards and, usually, all we had to do was give them the ball. But this time I took a pass from John and, when I looked up after going past a tackle, I saw that everyone was marked. So I hit it with my left foot from about forty yards out,' he said.

Here a beaming Johnny Morris interjected, as if offering a rational explanation for an unexplained phenomenon: 'He'd never kicked it with his left foot before, so no one knew what might happen!'

Unfazed, Anderson continued: 'I didn't see it go in the net because I fell over. But I heard this almighty roar so I thought, *Good God, I've scored*. I turned and started running.

I remember John Carey was standing there and he said, "Steady, son." If it hadn't been for him I think I might have run down the tunnel and out of the stadium.'

At centre half was the team's colossus, Allenby Chilton, whose prodigious physical strength was matched by exceptional leadership qualities. As Johnny Morris puts it: 'He controlled every move our defence made, directing the fullbacks and providing a focal point. He had something about him that made people follow him. You had to or he would give you a hiding. He was a genuinely hard man and I was proud to play alongside him.'

Charlie Mitten agreed, adding that Chilton should have won far more than his two England caps. 'It was simply ridiculous, but in those days there was a selection panel made up of club chairmen, and some very strange decisions were made.'

However, at least they recognised the merits of left half Henry Cockburn, who represented his country thirteen times. The one-time mill-fitter was a bundle of energy, both combative and constructive, and quite outstanding in the air for a fellow who stood only 5ft 5in before putting on his boots.

Charlie Mitten was delighted to have such a classy operator playing close behind him and he pays a warm tribute: 'He was right-footed but fitted in brilliantly on the left. When Henry got the ball I always knew I would be the next to touch it. There wasn't much of him, he was very light, but when he made a tackle his opponent knew all about it. He played an important part in what we achieved.'

For all the excellence of his rearguard, though, what rendered Matt Busby's class of 1948 truly exceptional was a forward line made in heaven, the celebrated Famous Five. Their football flowed and bubbled, by turns quick, subtle and powerful, and arguably they have never been equalled by another club forward line.

At outside right was Jimmy Delaney, one of a group of Scottish purchases made by Matt as the new manager of Manchester United, and the only one to be outstandingly successful. On the face of it Jimmy was not the most obvious transfer target, being thirty-one-years old at the time of his £4,000 arrival from Celtic in February 1946 and with a record of injury problems. But he confounded his doubters comprehensively, emerging as a key player for the next four and a half campaigns.

Charlie Mitten dubbed him '100 mph Jim' while Johnny Morris, his right-side partner, describes him as a pleasure to play with. 'He was the biggest bargain Matt ever struck. I could send him the ball without looking up; I always knew where he would be. Somehow, he always found plenty of room and if you can't knock the ball to a lad in acres of space then it's your own fault. He could move like lightning and he crossed well, too.'

One of the most telling testimonies to Delaney's worth was volunteered by Stan Pearson, shortly after the veteran's departure to Aberdeen. Said Stan: 'We were missing the old man because Jimmy used to give us heart.'

The number eight shirt was the property of Johnny Morris, who ranks among the finest post-war inside forwards – and with the likes of Raich Carter, Wilf Mannion, Len Shackleton and Stan Pearson on the scene that was saying something. There isn't an ounce of conceit in Johnny, but he is a realist, and when asked to sum up his own merits, he isn't shy: 'I can't say I had a weakness. I was a schemer who could pass the ball and nobody scared me. In tackles it was them or me.'

Admirably put, but he neglected to mention the beautiful control, the endless stamina and the intelligence to make the most of his myriad attributes. Whatever the rights or wrongs of his difference of opinion with Busby, United were the long-term losers when this sparky, effervescent, fiercely independent character became the first of the FA Cup-winning side to leave Old Trafford.

Weighing in at centre forward, but also capable of featuring wide on the left, was Jack Rowley, known as the 'Gunner'. Charlie Mitten was an admirer: 'I have never seen anybody better at shooting from distance. He would hit it from anywhere, especially with his left foot. Mind you, he needed clever players around him, but at United he had them.'

Johnny Morris adds: 'He could be a little selfish or we might have scored even more. I've even seen him shoot from the dead-ball line, when there was little hope of hitting the target, but he more than made up for that with the fantastic chances that he took. If anybody got in the way of his shot, likely as not he would end up in the net along with the ball.'

Some player, then, but if there was a poll of the '48-ers to decide who was the most influential member of the team, most probably that mantle would settle on the shoulders of the inside left, Stan Pearson. He was, they all agree, a lovely man and a masterful footballer: a beguiling mixture of visionary and multi-skilled technician – one of the most satisfyingly complete performers of his day. He provided brains and goals in equal measure, and his hallmark was accuracy: whether delivering raking cross-field passes, or dispensing delightful close-range flicks and glides, or finishing moves with predatory aplomb. He was a craftsman, as Johnny Morris agrees: 'Stan was a star. He wasn't a tackler, particularly, but he had a great head on his shoulders. He could send the ball through the tiniest of spaces to make openings for people. Sometimes he could thread a pass where one seemed impossible. He sized up his option in a split second and many people didn't realise just how marvellous he was, because he wasn't in the least bit showy. But ask any of us, we all knew. He made it easy for us. He was like a captain of the forward line.'

And then there was Cheeky Charlie Mitten, perhaps the most eye-catching of the quintet, an uncannily adept manipulator of the ball and a crowd-pleaser, sublime on the left wing. Not boastfully, but not shyly either, Charlie reminisce: 'There wasn't a fullback I couldn't beat. I had trickery and speed and a good left foot. My right was strictly for standing on. It hurt if I tried to kick with it!'

Morris lost in admiration for the ability of his old teammate, whose 100 per cent record at converting penalties was a trademark: 'I have never seen anyone kick a ball as accurately as Charlie. I could pass to him from a deep inside right position and set off for goal, knowing that by the time I arrived in the box the ball would arrive precisely on my head. I was amazed that he was never capped.'

As the Old Trafford reunion gathered momentum, aided by the eloquent presence of Busby Babe John Doherty and 1968 European Cup-winner David Sadler, the yarns of yesteryear abounded.

There was praise for Matt Busby, of course, and many an affectionate mention for his much-loved lieutenants, Jimmy Murphy, Bert Whalley and Tom Curry.

But as Ivan Ponting summed up: 'The most moving of all was the simple joy these men, these legends – Jack Crompton, Charlie Mitten, Johnny Morris and Johnny Anderson – had clearly known, in making their livings as Red Devils. To this humble observer, it was a privilege to be present.'

Chapter Nine

THE BUSBY BABES

—

Nothing lasts for ever, especially in football. Sir Alex Ferguson describes football as an evolution and says that the trick is to stay ahead of the game so that your next team is ready in the wings for the moment the current side, however successful, begins to falter.

Matt Busby grasped this concept right from the start of his career as manager of Manchester United, and from day one – as a soldier turned soccer manager just home from the war – he was planning for the future. It was always his dream to bring youngsters into his club, to bring them up in the ways of the game as he saw it, and that is exactly what he did. Even while he was working with the old guard and winning his first trophies, he was concentrating on the development and recruitment of boys he was bringing to Manchester, from as far afield as Scotland and especially the two Irelands.

United had always believed in encouraging youngsters and under Walter Crickmer, their long-serving secretary, who had acted as manager during the war, had set up the MUJAC, and they had also used the local works team at Goslings as a nursery for bringing on promising boys.

Louis Rocca, a key backroom Mr Fixit for United for many years, knew his way round the scouting system and in those important post-war years United made some canny appointments with Bob Bishop and Bob Harper in Belfast and Billy Behan in Dublin. Back home United lured Joe Armstrong from Manchester City and his job with the Post Office to become chief scout.

When it came to persuading anxious parents to let their footballing sons come to Old Trafford, especially when it involved coming across the Irish Sea, Joe was the proverbial uncle, a charmer, but sincere and principled with it. Busby had good men on his coaching staff, too, men like Bert Whalley, gifted and high-minded, Tom Curry the kindly trainer, Bill Inglis and good-living part-timers, like Jack Pauline who ran the junior teams.

Busby's assistant, Jimmy Murphy, was another who had a particular gift for raising young footballers as if they were his own sons. He always used to tell me: 'From little acorns big oak trees grow,' and you knew he had Duncan Edwards in mind, but more about Murphy and Edwards later.

The story of a vision that would take the football world by storm was just beginning, though for those who looked beyond the daring deeds of the first team you could already see the signs of something very special starting to emerge at Old Trafford.

The FA Youth Cup was launched in 1952 and not only did United win it that year, they went on to dominate the competition and win it for five successive seasons. The acorns were beginning to sprout, with only Wolves at that time cottoning on to the importance of developing your own players. It's commonplace now, but Busby along with Major Frank Buckley and Stan Cullis at Wolves were the first to plan so far ahead with real vigour.

United's youth team ran up some cricket scores against lesser teams in those early days, like beating Nantwich Town 23–0, and they also enjoyed an emphatic win in their first final, when they beat Wolves 7–1 in the home first leg, before drawing 2–2 at Molineux in the away leg.

The following year they inevitably met their big rivals, Wolves, again in the final. This was a much closer encounter: a 4–4 draw at Old Trafford was followed by a 1–0 win in the second leg. Players coming through at this stage included the likes of Bobby Charlton, Duncan Edwards, Eddie Colman, Wilf McGuinness, David Pegg and Albert Scanlon.

The fans knew they were seeing something special, in fact legends in the making, with the finals drawing crowds at Old Trafford of over 20,000. The discerning knew that they were watching the stars of tomorrow and that is exactly how it worked out when Matt Busby realised that his team of one-time solders was getting a bit long in the tooth.

Nevertheless, the football world still gasped when the manager, eager perhaps to blood the youngsters he had groomed, began to break up the old sweats. It must have been difficult for the medal-winning and much admired players, who had given Busby his first trophies, to accept that they had had their day. Indeed, it *was* tough, as John Aston admitted when he said: 'It was very disappointing for the players, who had brought the Championship to Old Trafford for the first time in over forty years, to have to give way to new men. But at the same time we were not blind to the fact that the Boss had also been busy creating a tremendously successful youth team that had won the FA Youth Cup five times off the reel when it was started.

'Matt Busby had also been at the club long enough to have established himself as a very far-seeing and shrewd manager. He had won the respect of all of us, which meant that it was easier for him to put over these new ideas. We just accepted the changes because when he said it was for the good of the club, we knew it was.'

The Championship cheers had hardly died down before Busby started to introduce the first of his Babes. The first youngsters to break in were wing half Jeff Whitefoot, the youngest ever to play in the League team (at sixteen years and 105 days, younger even than Duncan Edwards), David Pegg, a flying left winger, and inside forwards Dennis Viollet and John Doherty. Duncan Edwards, Jackie Blanchflower, Bill Foulkes and Eddie Lewis also made a bow. So, too, did the young office boy Les Olive, a goalkeeper, but later destined to play a much more important role in the club's affairs as secretary.

It was a period that was also notable for a relatively rare but nonetheless vital splash in the transfer market, with Busby paying the unusual fee of £29,999 to Barnsley for the dashing Tommy Taylor, in order to maintain the high scoring rate of his original side.

It was a time of change and experiment that was reflected in their First Division finishing position of eighth, with Arsenal the winners. But Busby knew what he was doing and the following season, 1953–54, saw players like Edwards, Taylor, Viollet, Whitefoot, Blanchflower and Foulkes become regulars and the team did a little better, to come fourth behind Wolves, the Champions.

The pivotal moment had come in late October after United had taken a team of youngsters to Kilmarnock for a friendly, as Busby explained: 'I walked the golf course thinking that this was the time to go the whole way. From the very start I had envisaged making my own players, having a kind of nursery, so that they could be trained in the kind of pattern I was trying to create for Manchester United.'

Busby was never afraid to spend money – as he had shown when he went for Delaney and Johnny Berry – whenever he felt there was a gap in his team that couldn't be filled to the right standard from his own supply chain. He wasn't afraid to break records, too. The £29,999 fee for Taylor was a record, so too was the £45,000 he paid to Sheffield Wednesday for Albert Quixall when he was rebuilding after Munich, and there were certainly raised eyebrows when he spent £115,000 to bring Denis Law home from exile in Italy with Torino. By and large though, he liked to bring on his own players, moulding their spirit and character to produce players who wore the red shirt with pride and determination.

His new team was still in a transitional stage, but new young players were coming through all the time, providing even fiercer competition for places.

Billy Whelan, the talented inside forward from the Republic of Ireland, was beginning to make a mark in the first team, while new boy Pegg found that he was in competition for the left wing spot with Albert Scanlon, another speedy winger. Mark Jones was in contention with Blanchflower for the centre half position.

Season 1954–55 saw them finish fifth, though only five points behind Chelsea, the new Champions. It was tight at the top. United were good. They were performing well but they still had to make the final leap. It came the following year, which coincided with the introduction of yet another talented kid in their ranks, the Salford wing half Eddie Colman. Now, only Roger Byrne and Johnny Berry remained from the team that had taken the title four years before. They made a slow start to the season. In fact they won only three of their opening eight matches, but they went up a gear in the New Year and lost only once between the start of January and the end of the season to take the title with sixty points.

The significance was that they were Champions with an average age of only twenty-two and they won it by a mile, eleven points ahead of runners-up Blackpool.

The medal winners were: Ray Wood, Bill Foulkes, Roger Byrne, Ian Greaves, Jeff Whitefoot, Eddie Colman, Mark Jones, Duncan Edwards, Johnny Berry, Jackie Blanchflower, John Doherty, Billy Whelan, Tommy Taylor, Dennis Viollet, David Pegg and Colin Webster.

One of the highlights of the season was the visit to Bolton in November, which pitted Nat Lofthouse against Tommy Taylor, in a match that was also notable for the debut of Eddie Colman. Tommy made his mark after only three minutes with a storming header from Johnny Berry's cross. Nat had the last word by scoring twice in Bolton's 3–1 win, but later said about his rival: 'This was Tommy at his best. The header he scored was world-class. The angle was awkward, but he rocketed the ball into our net. People were making out that this was some kind of showdown between Tommy and myself. Ridiculous. We were pals. Sure I wanted to keep the England spot. Who wouldn't? There was no animosity.'

Taylor was well into his scoring stride after missing the early part of the season with injury and he finished the season with twenty-five goals from thirty-three appearances. Dennis Viollet also had his eye in and from November onwards totalled twenty League goals from thirty-four games.

They were both on the scoresheet, naturally enough, when West Bromwich were beaten 4–1 on Christmas Eve and again two days later on Boxing Day, in a 5–1 win against Charlton Athletic. The return at Charlton the next day – three games in four days by the way – was lost 3–0, but there was still great excitement for the derby showdown against Manchester City at Old Trafford.

The gates were shut a good hour before kick-off, with thousands still outside. City scored first through Jack Dyson, but Taylor got the equaliser and Viollet the winner to avenge their Maine Road defeat earlier in the season.

United took a major step towards the Championship when they beat rivals Wolves 2–0 in February, with both goals scored by Taylor. By the end of March the Reds had slipped into a stunning run of form, emphasised by beating Newcastle 5–2 and then accounting for Huddersfield, who had been on a good run, 2–0. Taylor scored twice, to take his League scoring tally for United to one hundred.

United were in the driving seat for the title now and clinched it a couple of matches later when they entertained Blackpool, the other main challenger, at Old Trafford. It was another full house with the crowd a post-war record of 62,277. Blackpool scored early on, but a penalty from Johnny Berry, after John Doherty had been knocked over by the goalkeeper, and a winner from Taylor ten minutes from time, saw the Busby Babes clinch the title with two games to spare.

Matt Busby said: 'I never doubted their spirit or ability to pull through. It would have been a tragedy in football had they missed the title after playing so well through the hardest months of the winter. I have never known a spell so tense and hard, but this young team has done me proud. I am proud indeed of all my young players, right down from the First Division side to the colts.

'Two or three years ago, at the annual meeting of the club's shareholders, I said that United had youthful potential worth tens of thousands of pounds. I'm proud the boys have proved me right.

'I have, too, a grand board of directors, for which I am truly thankful; a wholehearted colleague in Walter Crickmer, fine coaches in Jimmy Murphy and Bert Whalley and front-line bulwarks in trainers Tom Curry and Bill Inglis. Ted Dalton, our physiotherapist, has also worked wonders on injured players. How eagerly United's younger players like Ian Greaves, Eddie Colman, Mark Jones, Duncan Edwards, Billy Whelan, John Doherty, Dennis Viollet and David Pegg have stepped up and taken their chances. And Tommy Taylor, who is only twenty-four, could be England's centre forward for years to come,' he added.

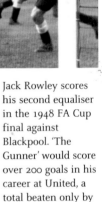

Jack Rowley scores his second equaliser in the 1948 FA Cup final against Blackpool. 'The Gunner' would score over 200 goals in his career at United, a total beaten only by Bobby Charlton and Denis Law. (*Popperfoto*)

Captain Johnny Carey lifts the trophy, with (left to right) John Aston, Allenby Chilton, Henry Cockburn, Charlie Mitten, Jack Crompton and Jack Rowley – it was the club's first major trophy since 1911. (*Empics*)

Johnny Carey, one of United's great captains, in action against Charlton in March 1949, shortly before he won the honour of Footballer of the Year. (*Empics*)

Fullback John Aston moves away from Portsmouth's Peter Harris. His career was eventually brought to an end by tuberculosis, but he was a very flexible talent who played in many positions for the club. (*Popperfoto*)

(Top left) Johnny Morris, star of the 1948 Cup-winning side, came up with a unique ploy to earn a transfer: he threatened to turn golf pro. (*Empics*)

(Top right) Jimmy Delaney, who was already 31 years old when Busby signed him from Celtic for a bargain £4,000 in 1946, still gave more than four years of superb service to the club. (*Empics*)

John Doherty's career was cut short by injury, but his role as chairman of the Former Players Association makes him a legend at Old Trafford. (*Empics*)

Inside forward Stan Pearson remains one of United's all-time leading goalscorers, and was a hugely popular character in the side. Here he is in action against Chelsea in 1949. (*Empics*)

Charlie Mitten scores United's equaliser in the 1949 FA Cup semi-final against Wolves. His United career was to end in controversy when he moved to Bogotá. (*Empics*)

Allenby Chilton comes away with the ball, with Bill Foulkes covering, during a match at Spurs in September 1953. Chilton was on a run of 165 successive League appearances before leaving the club in February 1955. (*Empics*)

Matt Busby's new generation: Busby, one of the first tracksuited managers, gives tips to Tommy Taylor, David Pegg and Dennis Viollet. (*Popperfoto*)

Johnny Berry, who scored both goals, with Matt Busby and Duncan Edwards (right) after United's 2–1 win over Bournemouth and Boscombe in the sixth round of the FA Cup in 1957. (*Empics*)

Champions! (Top) Roger Byrne with the trophy after the Busby Babes won the 1956 title by eleven points. (Above) Another year, another title: Johnny Berry, Bill Foulkes, Billy Whelan, Tommy Taylor and Bobby Charlton are among those celebrating with Matt Busby and Roger Byrne (in kit). (*Popperfoto*)

The European dream: (top) Tommy Taylor scores United's second goal on the way to a 3–0 win at Maine Road and an aggregate 6–5 victory over Athletico Bilbao; (above) that win set them up for a semi-final showdown with Real Madrid. Here Ray Wood saves from Alfredo Di Stefano, while Duncan Edwards, Roger Byrne and Jackie Blanchflower look on. (*Empics/Popperfoto*)

Chapter Ten

THE SMILING EXECUTIONER

T he Munich air crash would sadly put a stop to Tommy Taylor's career before he was even in his prime, as it did to the lives and dreams of most of his team-mates. At this stage, though, the Busby Babes were revelling in their youth and talent, bursting with ambition, energy and enthusiasm for the game of football.

Taylor arrived at Old Trafford in March 1953, signed from Barnsley for that record fee of £29,999 to avoid him being tagged the first £30,000 player, though in fact he did cost that figure, because Busby tipped the tea lady a pound for looking after them so well during protracted negotiations. For United were not the only club to be drawn to the possibilities of Barnsley's powerful young attack leader.

It was reckoned that there were around twenty clubs scouting the twenty-one-year-old boy who had been picked up by Barnsley from a local pub team, Smithies United. In fact, Jimmy Murphy said that, on one of the last occasions he had watched Taylor play at Barnsley, there were so many chairmen, managers and scouts watching, he thought it must be an extraordinary general meeting of the Football League.

Murphy said that his biggest problem was trying to persuade the player that he was good enough to play for Manchester United in the First Division, such was his natural modesty and contentment with his home-town, Second Division club.

'He didn't really want to leave Barnsley where everyone knew him. Eventually Matt Busby's charm won him over, and convinced him that if he came to Old Trafford to link up with the youngsters we had produced ourselves, the sky was the limit to his future in football.

'He had this mop of black hair and a perpetual smile on his face which prompted one sports writer of the time, George Follows, to christen him the "smiling executioner". He was one of the most sought-after players of all time. The more I saw of him, the more I realised he was a must for us.

'He was a superb mover, a man who possessed a grace and athleticism not normally found in tall men. He could crack a ball with either foot and when it came to heading, you could put him alongside Tommy Lawton and Nat Lofthouse. Of the centre forwards at that time, probably only John Charles could climb higher.'

Tommy Taylor was clearly a sensitive, nice guy, as is well illustrated by the experience of Laurie Cassidy, in a story recounted by Brian Hughes in his book, *The Tommy Taylor Story*.

Laurie had ten years on United's books after the war as a part-timer. He only made four League appearances, but he became an inspirational schoolteacher and an important figure in Manchester schools football. One day Laurie was training alongside Tommy Taylor when he was sent for by Matt

Busby. He recalls: 'Beside myself there was Cliff Birkett, Noel MacFarlane and Johnny Scott. When he had bad news to relay Matt would cough and clear his throat before continuing. "The directors have informed me that I have to release you players," he told us. It was obvious he didn't like this task, and he always said it was the directors who had made the decision. I accepted his explanation. He had youngsters coming along and he needed to play them. I'd had a good run and I was teaching.

'As I came out of the meeting, Tommy was outside doing something or other and I must have looked a little dejected. "What's wrong Laurie?" he asked. I explained what I had just been told by the boss, and Tommy was about to tear into the room to confront Matt about the club releasing me, until I stopped him. It was a lovely touch and I have never forgotten his gesture.

'The other lads were soon fixed up with other clubs. But to this day I often think about Tommy's spontaneous reaction to my being released by United. He was a thoughtful, caring person. I watched his career take off and was delighted when he received the praise that came his way. He was the best centre forward ever.'

Although it was in the classroom rather than on the football field, Laurie became a legend of another sort, at least to the hundreds of boys who passed through St Patrick's School in Collyhurst, Manchester. St Pat's was a soccer hotbed that produced players like Brian Kidd and Nobby Stiles for United and Colin Barlow for Manchester City, as well as a world boxing champion in Jackie Brown. Laurie was headmaster there for twenty-five years, was the manager of the Manchester Schools football team and served on their executive committee for most of his working life.

It didn't do Manchester United any harm having one of their old players in such an influential position in schools football. He certainly enjoyed the respect of the youngsters who passed through his school, as Brian Kidd recalls: 'After I had signed schoolboy forms for United, people began to put doubts in my mind and I didn't know what to do for the best. I remember one day in the playground the Head pulled me to one side. I was trembling in my boots, but he sorted me out, and if it had not been for such a caring headmaster, who gave me straight advice, I might easily have made a complete mess of things. He was always a father figure to the lads. You could always go to him. He had an easy, softly-softly manner, though when it was needed, he could be very tough. He had to be at times because it wasn't a school for cissies.'

So Manchester had football legends off the field as well as on it.

There was certainly no denying legendary status to Tommy Taylor. Two months after joining United he won the first of nineteen England caps, taking over from Nat Lofthouse as England's regular leader up front and scoring a fantastic sixteen goals. He played a leading role helping England qualify for the 1958 World Cup in Sweden, but was cut down before the tournament was played. For United he played 163 League games, scoring 112 goals, and scored 11 goals in 14 European appearances, again a phenomenal strike rate.

United had a wealth of inside forwards jostling to play alongside the big man, players like Dennis Viollet, Billy Whelan, Jackie Blanchflower before he was switched to centre half, and soon yet another up-and-coming youngster, Bobby Charlton.

It was Dennis, though, as the complete inside forward, who

made and scored goals with equal skill, who led the pack and won the right to play alongside Taylor. A former schoolboy international and captain of Manchester Boys, Viollet made a dashing partner for Taylor in the swashbuckling forward line of the mid-fifties, which won successive Championships and made a big impact in Europe.

His silky, sharp and stealthy approach made him a perfect foil until Munich took the life of Taylor and perhaps also took something from Viollet's game. Nevertheless, two seasons after Munich, in an attack featuring Bobby Charlton, Alex Dawson and Albert Quixall, he scored thirty-two League goals from just thirty-six appearances, a club record which still stands today.

It makes you wonder what he would have gone on to achieve with a maturing Taylor by his side, for United and perhaps for England, too. As it was, he won only two caps. Perhaps the selectors were put off by his seemingly slight physique. Thin faced and slim, he never appeared to have the strength for a robust game, but there was steel in that wiry frame and he had an electric burst of speed to go with an astute mind, good timing and an instinctive vision.

Or maybe the authorities thought him too carefree for the top level. In his early days especially, he lived life with a boldness that occasionally had embarrassing results, as I discovered to my cost writing a weekly column with him for the *Manchester Evening News*.

Between us we ventured to suggest that it was a shame Wolves rather than Manchester United had won the Championship in 1959 because it meant English football would be represented in Europe by what we considered to be a relatively primitive long-ball game, rather than by the culture of 'our' Manchester team.

The following day found us both summoned to Sir Matt Busby's office where we expected to be congratulated on our perceptive article, only to be handed the phone by the United manager to listen in turn to an irate Stan Cullis bellowing down it from Molineux and demanding an apology.

Dennis, as laid-back as ever and totally unruffled, took it all in his stride of course. 'Thanks very much for that, Scoop,' was all he said, with a big smile, after we had finally escaped the double-barrelled roasting.

Having grown up in Moss Side, in the shadow of Manchester City, it was no secret that as a boy, he had been a City supporter, but it did not prevent him giving Matt Busby excellent service – as well as a few headaches. He left Old Trafford after nine seasons but played nearly 200 more games for Tony Waddington at Stoke City, had a spell with Linfield in Northern Ireland and played for Ken Barnes, when his great Manchester City friend was manager of non-League Witton Albion. He enjoyed brief coaching spells at Preston and Crewe Alexandra before joining in the fashionable exodus to America, where he finally settled.

Despite his two paltry caps for England against Luxembourg and Hungary, his scoring record for United speaks for itself – 178 goals in 291 League and Cup appearances – and his former playing colleagues have nothing but admiration for his prowess.

John Doherty, team-mate and friend, said: 'He would always be in my all-time best United eleven. The lack of caps was an insult.'

Ken Barnes, the Manchester City captain and another admiring pal who played both with and against him, said: 'He was brilliant at timing his runs, which, together with great finishing, made him one of the best inside lefts in the game. He was so full of guile and craft and certainly a crafty blighter to play against.

'One of my most satisfying moments in football was when City played at Old Trafford in 1955 and we won 5–0. I would have liked Dennis to have suffered that one, but he was out with some injury, but then, of course, if he had been playing, we might not have got that result, because he was that kind of player!'

Towards the end of his life, Dennis had to battle with a brain tumour, and he fought it with the toughness he had always shown on the football field. He was already ill, but typically went against the doctor's advice when – as a guest of UEFA with the rest of Manchester United's air crash survivors – he insisted on attending the European Champions League final, when it was staged in Munich in 1997.

He wasn't well in Munich and he collapsed at the airport on his return to America and only his willpower kept him going during a long and debilitating illness. His death at the age of sixty-five was commemorated with a memorial service at Old Trafford and his ashes were scattered in the Stretford End goalmouth. His passing was also much mourned in America where he had lived for the last twenty-five years of his life. He was manager of Washington Diplomats from 1974 to 1977 and then became the highly regarded coach at Jacksonville University in Florida.

His successor at the university, a Serb, Aleksandar Mihailović, who had also played with him, said: 'He was regarded as the father of football in Florida. He went about his life in a way that was much younger than his years. He was a modest man, too, who never boasted about his deeds with

Manchester United. The only way you found out about what he had done with Matt Busby was by asking others. He never lived off his own exploits as a player.

'Like Sir Matt, he liked to encourage youth and his death was widely observed by the press, radio and on television.'

Dennis Viollet's escape from Munich did nothing to blunt a sharp sense of humour and a jaunty approach to life. Indeed those players who knew him before and after the crash say that afterwards he seemed to be even more determined to squeeze the last drop out of life.

As John Doherty, who grew up with him at Old Trafford, put it: 'The effect of Munich on his life was that he mustn't waste a minute of what was left.'

Chapter Eleven

THE GREATEST

—

The Busby Babes were essentially a team, but few would argue that the greatest of them all was Duncan Edwards.

Duncan was only twenty-one when he died from his injuries in Munich's Rechts der Isar Hospital, fifteen days after he had been dragged clear from the runway carnage.

But already he had more than made his mark, with the promise of so much more to come for club and country. He had won eighteen caps and after captaining the England Schoolboy team and the Under 23 side, he was regarded as the natural successor to Billy Wright at senior level.

He had been the youngest to play for England when he was given his first cap in April 1955, at the age of eighteen years and eight months, a debut marked by beating Scotland at Wembley 7–2. Walter Winterbottom, the England manager of that era, had no doubts about the player's international worth when he said: 'Duncan was a great footballer and he had the promise of being the greatest of his day. He played with tremendous joy and his spirit stimulated the whole England team. It was in the character and spirit of Duncan Edwards that I saw the true revival of British football.'

Jimmy Armfield who went on to captain England himself and who played with Duncan for Young England and the senior England team, as well as with him in Army teams during National Service, told me: 'With Duncan Edwards, Roger Byrne and Tommy Taylor in the team, I believe England would have at reached the final of the 1958 World Cup, and probably won it.

'The first thing that struck you about Duncan was his enormous build. He almost had the physique of a weightlifter and certainly when he played against people in his own age group, he appeared to carry almost twice their strength. Playing in the same team together I can still see this powerful figure stalking the dressing room and at the time I would think: "I'm glad he's playing for us."

'But it wasn't just power that made him a first-class player. He had fantastic technique. He was a brilliant footballer who never thought about losing. He was the perfect footballer, one of the finest all-round players I ever saw, or am ever likely to see. He deserves to be what he is, a football legend.'

His shooting was particularly eye-catching and even impressed the Germans. His shots had packed so much power when he had played in England's 3–1 win in Germany in 1956 that when United landed in West Berlin a few months later for the start of a pre-season tour, German fans were calling for 'Boom Boom'.

International football always posed a problem for his mentor at Old Trafford, Jimmy Murphy, who was manager of Wales, as well as Sir Matt Busby's assistant whose main job was the development of the young players.

Before one particular England–Wales match, Jimmy was running through the opposition detailing strengths and weaknesses. He referred to every England player bar Edwards, which left Reg Davies, the Welsh and Newcastle inside forward, feeling a little neglected, especially as he was in direct opposition to the United and England wing half.

'What about Edwards?' queried Davies.

Replied Murphy: 'There's nothing I could say which would help us. Just keep out of his way, son!'

Murphy regarded Duncan Edwards as simply the greatest and up to the time of his own death could barely mention Duncan's name without a tear coming to his eye.

Jimmy poignantly recalled in his book *United, Matt and Me*: 'If I shut my eyes I can see him now. Those pants hitched up, the wild leaps of boyish enthusiasm as he came running out of the tunnel, the tremendous power of his tackle – always fair but fearsome – the immense power on the ball.

'When I hear Mohammed Ali proclaim on television and radio: "I am the greatest" I have to smile. You see, the greatest of them all was an English footballer named Duncan Edwards. The real professional.

'Any manager lucky enough to have him had half a team. And that is why, when I heard the sad news of Duncan's death on the morning of Friday, 21 February 1958, I broke down and cried. The club and England had lost a great footballer. I had lost a friend, a very dear friend.

'From the first time I saw him as a boy of fourteen, he looked like and played with the assurance of a man, with legs like tree trunks, a deep and powerful chest and an unforgettable zest for the game. He played wing half, centre half, centre forward and inside forward with the consummate ease of a great player. He was never bothered where he played. He was quite simply a soccer Colossus.'

Born in Dudley, Worcestershire, United signed him as a schoolboy from under the noses of Wolves, much to the annoyance of Stan Cullis. United learned right from the start that despite being wooed by nearly every top club in the country, the team he wanted to join was Manchester United. Even so there was a last-minute scare when United's scout in the Midlands phoned to say that another club were stepping up their efforts to get his signature. The result was that United coach Bert Whalley drove through the night to the Edwards home in the early hours.

Duncan came down in his pyjamas to say: 'What's all the fuss about? I've already said Manchester United are the only club I want to join.'

True to his word, that's what he did, but it still left his local club, Wolves, frustrated and wondering whether money had changed hands. In later years Stan Cullis challenged Busby and asked him how he had managed to get the boy, when they thought he was lined up for Molineux. Matt explained it was simply the wish of Duncan himself; just as he had lost a Manchester youngster called Colin Booth, because Colin was simply a Wolves fan.

It must still have been difficult for Cullis to accept, especially when Edwards figured in the first ever FA Youth Cup competition in 1953 to help beat Wolves 9–3 on aggregate in the final.

The following season saw a repeat final with Duncan Edwards rubbing salt into the wound by scoring twice in a 5–4 aggregate win. By the time of the third season Edwards was well established in United's first team, but he liked nothing better than turning out with his peers and returned to the junior side to help notch up a crushing 7–1 victory against West Bromwich over two legs in the final.

He was almost unstoppable at youth level and in one tie at Chelsea, Jimmy Murphy had issued pre-match instructions that they should play their normal game without funnelling everything to their star. Then at half-time when they were a goal down he told them to forget what he had said and that they should look to give Duncan the ball. They did and he scored twice for a 2–1 win. It was true Roy of the Rovers stuff.

Jimmy Murphy also liked to recall a youth tie at Charlton, when he was being given some stick by a Cockney fan in the face of a relatively quiet performance from Duncan.

'Where is he? We ain't seen him, mate,' shouted the home fan, but even as he spoke Edwards hit one from forty yards and as it sailed into the Charlton net Murphy was able to turn round and declare: 'There, my friend, is Duncan Edwards!'

After Jeff Whitefoot by a few weeks, he was the youngest player to appear in the First Division, when United gave him his League debut against Cardiff City at Old Trafford on 4 April 1953, at the tender age of sixteen years and 185 days.

United lost 4–1 and he didn't play again that season, but the following year he strode majestically into action as Sir Matt Busby unveiled the rest of his Busby Babes. He played superbly as Busby's freshly built young side won the Championship in the successive years of 1956 and 1957. He also scored in United's remarkable 5–4 First Division win at Arsenal, just before the team flew out to Belgrade for their fateful European Cup quarter-final against Red Star.

It was tragically his last game on English soil, but certainly a memorable one with Duncan scoring a typical goal to give United the lead. Busby's boys led 3–0 at the break but Arsenal fought back, only for the visitors to step up another gear to win a match also notable for the introduction of two more young-sters, wingers Albert Scanlon and Kenny Morgans.

A bigger than life bronze statue now stands in the market place in his home town of Dudley, and in the nearby St Francis Church there are two stained-glass windows, unveiled by Sir Matt Busby in 1961, dedicated to his lasting memory. For those who saw him play, though, the memories of this stunning young player remain even more vividly.

Sir Bobby Charlton, like Jimmy Armfield and Duncan him-self, another National Service soldier, wrote about him in his book *My Soccer Life*: 'I remember playing with him once in an Army Cup tie. We were 4–2 down with the game nearly over. So Duncan switched to centre forward. In ten minutes he scored four and we won 7–4. It was a relatively unimportant match but it supplies the key to his genius. For Duncan, you see, there was no such thing as an unimportant match. In one season he played nearly a hundred games for United, England and the Army – and he gave a hundred per cent in the lot.

'I don't say he intended to. There were probably small-time Army games when he thought he would have a quiet cruise through – just keep out of trouble and not over tire himself for the next international or League match. But once the game started everything else went out of his mind. He ran and tack-led and surged through as if his reputation depended upon it. Whether it was at Wembley or on a bumpy pitch behind the barracks, he became immersed in it.'

Bobby remembers when he joined United as a youngster and met Jimmy Murphy for the first time, and found his new boss talking non-stop about the attributes of a chap called Edwards.

'I wondered at the time why Jimmy was bothering with me if this Edwards was so good. Later I understood why he couldn't stop talking about him. He was the greatest. I see him in my mind's eye and wonder that anyone should have so much talent. He had the sort of build a boxer pines for. He was a shade under six feet and weighed about 13 and a half stone. He was a hard, tough man in the tackle, but he was also a shrewd intelligent player.

'His other exceptional quality was that he always liked to be winning or saving matches. He had a shot that could burst through the best goalkeeper's hands, yet when the pressure was on in his own goalmouth, he would be back there battling away. He had that sort of speed that made that possible and ensure he was never caught out of position. One minute he would be clearing off his line, the next surging through at the other end. He was out on his own at left half, and a First Division player in every other position.'

Sir Bobby Robson also paid tribute at his passing: 'Duncan was unique. I played with him for England, just a kid really, but he was a terrific player, going through midfield like a battleship. As well as being strong, tough and quick, he was a great header of the ball, two-footed and liked to tackle. He could hit the diagonal passes and had a strong shot. He would be worth a fortune in today's game.'

After playing against Red Star in Belgrade for a 3–3 draw that put the Reds into the semi-finals of the European Cup, the weather was so bad that Duncan, always thoughtful and caring, sent a telegram to his landlady in Gorse Avenue, Stretford, saying: 'All flights cancelled flying tomorrow – Duncan.'

Tragically they did fly and Duncan Edwards fought bravely for his life. Frank Taylor of the *News Chronicle*, the only surviving journalist, said it was only Duncan's stupendous spirit that had kept him battling for as long as he did.

One of the doctors at the Rechts der Isar Hospital said afterwards: 'I have seen death many, many times, but not like this. In all my years I have never seen a hospital staff so upset. This boy we have never seen before, he comes to our hospital – but he is so young, so strong, and so brave. Ach, but he had no chance.'

As Frank Taylor wrote: 'There were many tears that day in Munich, and far beyond, for a boy who had taken the world of sport by storm; who epitomized the power and zest and all that's best in British sport. A worthy young sports idol for the youth of the nation. Duncan Edwards was unforgettable. So long, Dunc. It was great while it lasted.'

Chapter Twelve

STRENGTH IN DEPTH

———

Manchester United had strength in depth with their Busby Babes, and though their stars were legendary, quality ran right through their team. Not one of them could afford to think he was safe because the competition for places was fierce.

One of the most attractive personalities and most versatile was Jackie Blanchflower, brother of Danny of Spurs fame. He was already a Northern Ireland schoolboy international when he arrived at Old Trafford from Belfast, to begin a career which started with cleaning Charlie Mitten's boots.

By the time he was twenty-two though, he had won a League Championship medal, starting out as an inside forward, but also playing at centre half until Mark Jones began to edge him out. The following season he proved even more versatile, taking over as an emergency goalkeeper in the 1957 FA Cup final against Aston Villa following injury to Ray Wood. United lost but not through any fault of the goalkeeper.

He won twelve caps for Northern Ireland, playing in a

successful team with his brother Danny that qualified for the World Cup finals in Sweden in 1958.

He didn't play against Red Star in Belgrade but travelled as a reserve and was seriously injured in the crash on the way home. Harry Gregg found him lying on the runway and used his tie to stop the bleeding from his mangled arm, but broken ribs and a smashed pelvis meant he never played football again.

In later life Jackie had mixed emotions about the crash and I remember him explaining to me on one of the anniversaries of the tragedy: 'I have one set of feelings I keep to myself and another when I am asked. My truth probably lies somewhere in between. The thing is that Munich has become a legend and I must admit I have tired of the pathos of it. My memories now, years later, are of all those fit young men so full of life.

'As a team we were unbelievably close and happy, and those are the times I like to remember now. When we had the twenty-fifth anniversary I was interviewed by television and recalled some of the humorous experiences we had shared, but they were cut out. They wanted only the sadness.

'I don't want to forget, especially the happy times we all shared. We will never see them grow old of course. They will never be fat and balding like I'm going to be. All the survivors have their different memories and ideas. Most of us have come to accept things. Some people think I am bitter, but I'm not really. I'm overweight and unfit, but I'm all right. There are the odd twinges and pains but I'm not complaining.'

Blanchflower's former team-mates not only remember him for his stylish football and his warm personality, but for his bravery at the end of his life. His spirit was there for all to see when he attended a charity match at Old Trafford on the fortieth anniversary of the Munich crash, to raise money for the survivors and dependants.

Jackie had been fighting a losing battle with cancer and complications, but he was determined to make the match and meet up again with fellow survivors, especially Harry Gregg, a particular pal and of course his saviour on that snow-covered runway.

Jackie perhaps also had in mind the even more unfortunate players who didn't come back at all, like Tommy Taylor, who had been best man at his wedding.

Jackie died aged sixty-five, a fortnight after the commemorative match, and up until a month before that game he was still keeping appointments as an after-dinner speaker. He had had a variety of jobs after football ranging from keeping a pub to a betting shop, but eventually honed an ability to entertain as a speaker. It was his answer to his wrecked football career at the age of twenty-five. He developed a brilliantly droll and funny act that drew not just on his experience as a footballer but also on a natural Irish wit that was sharp and ironic.

Jean Blanchflower, his wife of forty-two years and herself once in the entertainment business as a singer and popular comedienne, told me at the funeral: 'Jackie had bookings through into the next year, but right to the end as he lay in bed his thoughts were about how he didn't want to let anyone down. He was determined to get to the Munich match, despite being so very poorly. I shall miss him terribly. Maybe not everyone liked him as a footballer, but I never came across anyone who didn't like him as a person. I really regret he didn't get past retirement age, but he couldn't have gone on any longer,' she added.

United lost another of their crash survivors with the death

in 2002 of Ray Wood from a heart attack at the age of seventy-one. Ray was signed from Darlington for £5,000 in 1949 as cover for Jack Crompton and he went on to displace Jack to win Championship medals in 1956 and 1957 playing behind the Busby Babes. Born in the North East at Hebburn, he played 178 League games for United and won three England caps.

It was in the FA Cup, though, where he played himself into the club's history as a legend by becoming the central figure in the drama at Wembley when Aston Villa's Peter McParland crashed into him to leave him with a broken cheekbone and the club's dream of a League and Cup double in ruins.

The game was only six minutes old. Jackie Blanchflower went into goal, and though Ray came back on later in the game, United lost 2–1 with McParland ironically the scorer of the two Villa goals.

As Bobby Charlton said in his book: 'I cannot believe Villa would have won had we stayed a complete unit, not the way we were playing that season.'

Ray lost his place as the number one keeper when Matt Busby signed Harry Gregg shortly before the Munich crash. Ray stayed in the squad which meant he travelled to Belgrade, and head injuries from the crash hampered his attempts to regain his place in the team.

He moved to Huddersfield after winning his second Championship medal in a bid for first-team football, and also played for Bradford City and Barnsley, before trying his luck in America. Perhaps that was where he picked up his wandering ways, because after qualifying as an FA coach he spent the next twenty-five years travelling the world and logging up an amazing catalogue of jobs.

When United were winning the European Cup in 1968, Ray

was coaching in the United States. Then he had nearly three years in Cyprus, a year in Greece, one in Kuwait, four in Kenya, six months in Canada, three and a half years in the United Arab Republic, and assorted tours for the British Council in Zambia.

He received most of the appointments through recommendations from the Football Association who knew him as a qualified, reliable and gifted coach who liked globetrotting.

'I didn't set out to work abroad, but one job just led to another and once I had retired from playing, I still needed to work. I enjoyed all the various places, except Greece, where they were too busy selling games and forgetting to pay me which wasn't much fun.

'I suppose the high spot was in Kenya where I won the League three times and the Cup once. I also won the Eastern Central National Championship with Kenya in 1975,' he told me a few years ago on one of his trips to Manchester, as an enthusiastic member of the Former Players Association.

A keen golfer, he settled eventually in Bexhill, Sussex, where he worked in a gentleman's outfitters, but he always remembered with particular warmth the friendship he shared in his United days with Jeff Whitefoot, Dennis Viollet and Mark Jones. He recalled a favourite story: 'The four of us used to do the pools and when one week we came up with twenty-three points we thought we had won a fortune. We booked a taxi and a slap-up meal at the Midland Hotel, which for footballers in those days was doing it grand. Matt Busby got to hear about it and sent for us. I think he thought we might not bother with the next game. He needn't have worried. It turned out we had to share £28 and we had to cancel the dinner.'

No mention of the Busby Babe legends would be complete without paying tribute to the captain, Roger Byrne, who didn't know when he died at Munich that his wife, Joy, was expecting their first child, who would be called Roger in loving memory of his dad.

Born locally in Gorton, Roger went to Burnage Grammar School and did two years' National Service in the RAF before joining United as an outside left, only to make his debut in 1951 at left back. Busby didn't hesitate though to move Roger back to the wing when John Aston returned from injury. Roger played brilliantly to score seven goals in the last six games on the run-in for the 1952 Championship. It was a decisive contribution that clinched the title.

Naturally, Byrne was kept on the wing for the start of the following season, but he didn't like it and asked for a transfer.

Roger was always his own man and at times would stand up to Busby. The pair of them had a curious relationship, with Roger unafraid of his boss, but there was also a mutual respect and Busby admired his player's leadership qualities and his readiness to argue for what he believed in.

The result was that Byrne was returned to fullback where he steadily built a reputation as a fast and intelligent defender who was also prepared to use his wing experience and speed to raid down his flank. As the title-winning team began to break up Roger represented the future, and as the younger players came into the team, they found him to be a natural leader. A year after Johnny Carey had retired Roger was officially made captain and his influence on the Busby Babes was incalculable.

As Albert Scanlon put it: 'The man I admired most at United was Roger Byrne. I had always been a little afraid of our previous captain, Johnny Carey, and I never spoke to him unless he spoke to me first. It was quite different with dear old

Roger. Although he was just as much a gentleman, we always felt that Roger understood us as well as he understood football. One of the things that I think is wrong with football today is that there doesn't seem to be discipline and respect commanded by men like Roger.'

Roger Byrne was the right man in the right place at the right time, as Busby's boys gradually replaced the old guard, and he was young enough, of course, to form the bridge between the 1952 and 1956 Championship-winning teams. Around the time he was appointed captain at Old Trafford, he was selected for England against Scotland for the first of thirty-three consecutive caps, and as Jimmy Armfield pointed out earlier, he would have made a natural successor to Billy Wright as the England skipper.

Alas, it was not to be as tragedy swept through the Busby Babes, with Billy Whelan another of the bright young talents to perish.

Billy, or Liam as he was called back in his native Dublin, joined as an eighteen-year old from Home Farm: another club that acted as a nursery for United. He soon won a place in the team and as the Busby Babes grew in confidence to win the Championship for a second time, he was the team's leading scorer with twenty-six League goals – even more than Tommy Taylor. He was yet another player with a one-in-two scoring rate, overall netting forty-three goals from seventy-nine League appearances.

Billy was shy and in the, at times, rough, tough world of professional football, stood out as a religious young man who might well have entered the priesthood. Team-mates recall that on the third and fatal attempt to take off at Munich, Liam Whelan was heard to say that if the worst happened then he was ready, and they have no doubt that meeting his Maker was what he had in mind.

Heartbreakingly, that was his fate, along with another popular figure, the cheeky, chubby-looking Eddie Colman from Archie Street in Salford. He was especially young looking, so much so that when he tried to go through the players' entrance at Bloomfield Road for a match against Blackpool one day, the gateman wouldn't let him through and directed him to the kids' turnstile.

If ever a youngster was destined to become a legend it was Eddie Colman, who had such a delightful body swerve that he had been dubbed 'Snake Hips'. He won a Championship medal in 1956, but alas, he died at twenty-one after playing only eighty-five League games.

Chapter Thirteen

THE CHAIRMAN

S ome fifty years ago, John Doherty was one of Matt Busby's most likely lads. Despite growing up in the illustrious company of Duncan Edwards, Bobby Charlton, Dennis Viollet and the rest, the bright-eyed Mancunian never looked like being overshadowed, so rich and varied were his own exquisite gifts.

John was an inside forward whose touch on the ball, with either foot, was gloriously assured. He could pass with unerring accuracy and was blessed with the sharp intelligence to make that talent tell. To cap it all, he packed a shot of sudden, savage power.

Thus it appeared probable that he would illuminate the upper echelons of the English game for the foreseeable future. Fate, though, had other ideas, intervening in the shape of a recurring knee injury, which caused John to miss the first FA Youth Cup final in 1953.

John had been part of a free-scoring forward line, which included Irish right winger Noel McFarlane, locally born centre forward Eddie Lewis, David Pegg at inside left and Albert

Scanlon on the left flank. To replace John at inside right, Busby enlisted a replacement from the Home Farm club of Dublin, a courteous, quietly spoken fellow by the name of Billy Whelan.

Duly they defeated Wolves, the newcomer excelled and scored in both legs, and the eighteen-year-old Doherty, who had made his senior debut along with Pegg at home to Middlesbrough earlier in the season, was left to embark on a lengthy period of recuperation. While Billy progressed smoothly towards the status of first-team regular, John's knee problems never cleared up fully and he was condemned to the overwhelming frustrations of a stop–start career.

Indeed, so serious was his condition that he was invalided out of National Service in the RAF, but he refused to give up and resurfaced at First Division level in the autumn of 1955. Come mid-season he earned a settled run in the side, at the expense of Jackie Blanchflower, and he finished the campaign with sixteen League appearances to his name, enough to qualify on merit for a Championship medal.

That should have been the springboard for serial achievement, but that troublesome knee flared up again and he returned to the sidelines. Then John, a forthright fellow, experienced a difference of opinion with his manager that culminated in a £6,500 transfer to Leicester City in October 1957.

At Filbert Street he impressed in a dozen First Division outings before breaking down again, and he was in hospital recovering from yet another operation when he learned of the Munich air disaster. Among those who died was the lad who had replaced John four years earlier, Billy Whelan.

Looking back, the sixty-six-year-old chairman of the Association of Former Manchester United Players is admirably philosophical about his premature exit from the game he continues to love: 'My knee injury stopped me from going on, but I like to be positive. It might easily have finished me at eighteen, but I managed another five. Of course, in today's world, with all the medical advances there have been, the injury would have barely interrupted my career, but there's no point in dwelling on that.

'After all, if I'd been fully fit, and if I'd never left United, who knows how the pages of my personal history might have been rewritten. For a start, I might have been on that plane. So although I was unlucky in one respect, if I look at the broader picture, I can say I've been extremely fortunate. At least I've had a life. There's no way I'm complaining.'

After leaving Leicester in the summer of 1958, John became player-manager of Rugby Town and served various other non-League clubs, including Bangor City as team boss in the late sixties.

Thereafter, he gained wide experience in the field of finance, served Burnley as chief scout for a spell in the 1980s, and then went on to succeed in insurance and sports promotion. In addition, he has been a moving force in the Association of Former Manchester United Players, relishing his involvement as a founder member, and continuing as chairman because the committee simply won't let him give up.

You might think that John Doherty's relatively brief playing career with United barely qualifies him for inclusion as a legend, but in my book, and if you talk to his former colleagues, the 'Chairman', as they call him, has contributed a great deal to Manchester United as the leader of the old boys' Association. Along with committee men like secretary David Sadler and treasurer Warren Bradley, the Association has raised thousands of pounds for charity and provided an organisation that keeps old team-mates in touch and helps those who fall on hard times. Injuries suffered in youth have a nasty habit of catching up with old pros in later years and there are a number who have cause to be grateful to their Association for timely assistance.

Nobody has a better knowledge of those who have played in a red shirt. Indeed he recently published a book, *The Insider's Guide to Manchester United*, a pithy summing up of the strengths and weakness of the 348 players who have played for United since the war.

Naturally he has a special affection for his own era and as he casts his mind back and assesses Busby's legends he says: 'Ray Wood was a good 'keeper, not a great one, but very, very good. He was a wonderful shot-stopper with safe hands and his ability was recognised by his three England caps. If he had a weakness it was in collecting crosses. He reached his peak in the 1955–56 and 1956–57 Championship seasons, but then the team had a bad run and he was replaced by Harry Gregg.

'I didn't play with Harry at United, but I lined up for Leicester against him on the day he made his debut and I saw plenty of him. Now, I thought he *was* a great goalkeeper, a bit before his time in that he commanded his area. The United defence wasn't used to a 'keeper charging off his line and pushing everyone out of the way as he claimed the ball. If anybody got in his way, he'd practically chin them! He was voted the best 'keeper in the 1958 World Cup finals for his efforts with Northern Ireland and I can understand why. Sadly, Harry was cursed by suffering injuries at the wrong times. United took the title and the FA Cup while he was at Old Trafford but he never won a medal.

'Bill Foulkes never stepped outside the top division and

Matt Busby selected him nearly 700 times, so that speaks for itself. Essentially Bill was a mightily effective defender who stopped opponents from playing. He was a part-timer, working in a mine, when he started at United, and he was big and strong. He wasn't the best passer, but he didn't need to be, because when he got the ball he would give it, simply and sensibly, to the nearest red shirt. He played at right back in the early days but then became a centre half a little while after Munich. That position suited him because he was at his best with the ball coming on to him. Matt thought a great deal of Bill, knowing he could trust him in any job he was asked to do.

'Roger Byrne was totally different from Bill. Roger personified class. He played left back off his right foot, he wasn't a tackler and he wasn't a header of the ball, but he was as fine a left back as I've ever seen. In fact, his brain and his pace made him as good as there has been. Eventually, Roger became a wonderful skipper of Manchester United, like Johnny Carey before him. The lovely thing was that both Roger and Johnny had truly great teams to captain.

'Geoff Bent was a natural left back. If he had been promoted to the first team, it would have allowed Roger to play on the right, his own natural side. A lot of people expected it to happen, but it never did. At any other club but United, Geoff would have been a regular. He was a fine all-round footballer and very hard. He was highly unfortunate not to play more games at the top level.

'Ian Greaves earned a title medal by keeping Bill Foulkes out at the back end of the 1955–56 season. At that point, Ian really looked the part. He was big and strong, he could pass the ball and he was fairly quick. But Foulkes reclaimed his place at the start of the next campaign and that was it for Ian, until he returned to the team after Munich. Perhaps he wasn't quite as ruthless as Bill, but who was?

'Eddie Colman and Jeff Whitefoot were both gifted right halves, but of vividly contrasting styles. I played with Eddie in the youth team, and he was different. He was a special talent, but I'm not sure that he would have flourished anywhere but with Manchester United at that time. He needed top players with him and I don't think he could have attempted to be the Eddie Colman he was if he had been condemned to play in a poor team. Old Trafford was made to measure for Eddie. He came into what was already a very good side with Jeff Whitefoot at right half and, to be fair to Jeff, it would have remained a good side if he had stayed there. United didn't give possession away and that suited Eddie. Jeff was a different type of footballer, a superb passer. Eddie was more a performer on the ball, a man for the mazy dribble which the crowds loved. Oh, Eddie could pass the ball smartly enough, of course, but he couldn't deliver it forty or fifty yards off both feet like Jeff Whitefoot, a thoroughbred player who was immensely unfortunate to lose his place, but football is full of that.

'He proved what a fine performer he was in his long spell at Nottingham Forest, who he helped to win the FA Cup in 1959. A lot of people would have liked him back after Munich, but perhaps he felt he was best advised to remain elsewhere, having made a fresh start.

'Jackie Blanchflower made his debut as a left half against Liverpool (on the day that Roger Byrne was called up) but he suffered a cartilage injury in training the following week and didn't play in the first team for a long time afterwards. Eventually he returned as an inside right and scored quite a few goals. Then he made a third debut as a centre half and he demonstrated his versatility even more vividly as an emergency goalkeeper when Ray Wood was injured in the 1957 FA Cup final. Jackie was a marvellous all-rounder. He had two fine feet, he was good in the air and had a sharp footballing brain, but he wasn't blessed with much pace. Perhaps left half was his natural position, but he did a splendid job in the other roles. In fact, centre half suited him because it gave him a bit more time. He wasn't as commanding as big Mark Jones, because he was several inches shorter, but he had more all-round quality as a player. Whether he was better than Mark at centre half is difficult to say.

'Certainly Mark was a magnificent person. I named my first son after him because he was a super lad and a good footballer, so dominant in the air, and at times we thought he could have been an England player. But for the Munich crash, in which he died, he might have been because he was still a young fellow and Billy Wright was approaching the end of his career.

'Ronnie Cope was another centre half, an England schoolboy international who joined at the same time as me. Ronnie was a lovely lad and we are great pals to this day, but the competition he faced in the centre of defence was terrifying. When he arrived there was Allenby Chilton in the first team, Sammy Lynn in the reserves and Mark Jones in the A team, and that's without mentioning Jackie Blanchflower. Anyone could be forgiven for thinking, "Why did he choose to come to Old Trafford?" Though he did well for the club after Munich, before joining Luton.

'It was always obvious that Duncan Edwards was going to be an exceptional player, a big, strong lad with good feet, powerful in the air and it was difficult to pinpoint a weakness in his game. You'd have to say he was magnificent, and consistently so. He was so fit and possessed such an incredible appetite for the game. More than anything else, he wanted to play. He barely suffered an injury before Munich, God bless him, and it makes me think, when I might be feeling sorry for myself, that I'm sure Duncan would have liked to have had an injury, like me, and lived. It could be said that he paid dearly for his love affair with the game. I saw him as a future captain of United and England. He had the stature; he was a commanding person with a presence about him and a certain arrogance in his game, although arrogance played no part in his personality when he was not on the pitch.

'He captained England Schoolboys and won two full caps as a combative wing half, but Wilf McGuinness wasn't a Duncan Edwards, and he knew that. Wilf was a hustler and a tackler, with a heart like a lion. He would challenge for anything, and that was worth a lot, but he could do nothing about the broken leg that cut short his playing career. Freddie Goodwin was also a wing half who came to Old Trafford out of the forces and out of the blue, a fine passer and a thinker who brought a touch of vision to his game. He was behind an awful lot of players in the pecking order, though, and didn't claim a first-team place until after Munich.

'Johnny Berry, now here was one exceptionally fine player, tough as old boots, quick as lightning and extremely skilful. Fullbacks could frighten many wingers out of a game, but they could never frighten Johnny. He was always ready to chase back and challenge, and he had so much courage. Johnny was awarded a handful of international caps, but he was unlucky to coincide with the likes of Stan Matthews and Tom Finney. There were plenty of other top wingers, too, such as Johnny Hancocks and Jimmy Mullen of Wolves and Peter Harris at

Portsmouth. Matt bought Johnny from Birmingham after he had played well against us in an FA Cup tie and he was an unqualified success. In fact, when you're picking a best-ever United team, Johnny Berry must be knocking on the door. He had lost his place to Kenny Morgans at the time of Munich, and he had reached his thirties, but I can't imagine that he was washed up. But for his injuries in the crash, I think Johnny would have been back.

'Kenny Morgans did amazingly well to oust a classy performer like Berry. He was just a kid, but he was a tricky little customer who had something about him. He was barely on the scene, not even in the reserves, when I left in October 1957 and it was hard to imagine him making the sort of progress necessary to remove Johnny. But he made a burst, came from nowhere to get ahead of Colin Webster and Alex Dawson, he impressed everyone.

'Both David Pegg and Albert Scanlon were marvellous wingers who were immensely effective. I made my debut with Dave – at home to Middlesbrough in December 1952 – a tricky, dribbling outside left who wanted to drop a shoulder and slip past his fullback. I played with Albert for Manchester Boys in the English Schools Shield final. He was more direct, tending to receive the ball, run past his defender and get in a cross. He was a flier, but sometimes he could be a bit naive in his approach. On their day both were good enough for England. Dave got one full cap and Albert made the Under 23s, but then never developed as many people expected despite scoring a lot of goals in his first full season after surviving Munich. I suppose Bobby Charlton's shift to outside left didn't help him. It's difficult to separate them. In the youth team the problem was solved by playing Albert on the wing and Dave at inside left.

'In my opinion, Dennis Viollet was as good as anyone who has played since the war. When he started up front alongside Tommy Taylor, his scoring record was fantastic. Then, after he had lived through Munich, he played in a slightly deeper position and broke Jack Rowley's club goal-scoring record for a season, by piling up thirty-two in thirty-six games during 1959–60. At that time he was playing at centre forward with Albert Quixall and Bobby Charlton on either side of him. It amazed me that Dennis won only two England caps, and that he wasn't picked until two years after Munich. He should have been a regular to line up alongside Tommy. Instead England chose people like Derek Kevan and Johnny Nicholls of West Bromwich Albion. No disrespect to those lads, but it made me want to weep. Dennis had pace, touch, a brilliant brain and he wasn't afraid to stick his foot in. He wasn't the best striker or header of a ball, but that made no difference. Quite simply, he was a magnificent player and he would always be a certainty for my best ever United team.

'One of greatest centre forwards ever, Tommy Taylor, was a majestic footballer, yet strangely underrated. He took some stick from the press, especially from Henry Rose of the *Daily Express*, who once wrote that if Tommy Taylor could play, then he would eat his hat. It was strange that they should die together at Munich. A measure of Tommy's achievement is that, by the time of the tragedy, he had ousted Nat Lofthouse from the England side. I wasn't surprised because Tommy was a better all-round player than Nat, fantastic in the air, and the only man who could be compared to the great Tommy Lawton. His scoring record was phenomenal, something like two goals for every three matches he played for United, and sixteen in nineteen outings for England. People said his control let him down, but that was rubbish. You didn't finish with his sort of record if you had poor feet. He had a wonderful engine, too, and if his team was under the collar he would roam and hold the ball while his defence regrouped and reorganised, the perfect team man in every way.

'Billy Whelan was an Irish inside forward blessed with wonderful skills which were suited to the team. He was a thoroughbred and although he could look a bit awkward on the ball and wasn't the quickest, he had a brilliant touch and was a superb dribbler. He scored a lot of goals, too, and if only he'd had pace, there would have been no limit to his potential.

'In 1956–57, his last full season before he lost his life in the crash, he was particularly prolific, finishing as the club's top scorer in League games with a tally of twenty-six. Counting his FA Cup and European goals, he totalled thirty-three. Nevertheless, for all Billy's success, he had lost his place to Bobby Charlton at the time of Munich and I think he would have been unlikely to win it back. For all his assets, I wouldn't have put Billy in Bobby's class.

'There's no point in lingering too long on Bobby Charlton because so much has been written about him already. In the 1950s he was seen as a front player, a scoring inside forward, and he was very good at it. In the years that followed he enjoyed a glorious international career as a midfielder, such was his fabulous talent. Bobby had an attribute that nobody can give or teach, and that's pace. He had great feet, too, and contrary to what people think, he was good in the air. He had the lot.

'Colin Webster was a utility forward who played for Wales in the 1958 World Cup finals. He never had a regular first-team place at United, but he was useful to bring in when reinforcements were needed. He was quick, a decent a goal-scorer and he worked hard.

'Alex Dawson came as an outside right, but then moved into the middle. A big strong lad, he did very well for United after Munich. He had an excellent scoring record and was a decent player, but eventually moved on. Eddie Lewis was a tall, muscular Mancunian who let nobody down when he sampled First Division life as a centre forward, before the arrival of Tommy Taylor. He scored a few goals – I believe it was seven in ten games in 1952–53 – and later served Preston and West Ham in the same position. But it was as a fullback with Leyton Orient that he enjoyed his greatest success, helping them to reach the top division under the management of Johnny Carey in season 1961–62.'

Chapter Fourteen

INTO EUROPE

The Babes were on the march and the reigning champions had the bit between their teeth as they raced into action the following season and found themselves challenging for a treble of League, FA Cup and Europe!

Winning the 1956 Championship had seen them invited by UEFA to compete in the European Cup, and although Chelsea had turned down a similar invitation the previous year under advice from the insular Football League, Matt Busby was a man of vision.

Busby explained: 'I was very keen on the idea and at one of our board meetings early in May 1956, Harold Hardman the chairman asked me if I thought it wise that the club should go in for the added commitment. My reply was: "Well, Mr Chairman, football has become a world game. It no longer belongs exclusively to England, Scotland and the British Isles. This is where the future of the game lies." Mr Hardman replied: "All right, if that's what you really feel." I said: "Yes, I do, I think we should try it."'

It was after this simple exchange of views that Manchester

United launched themselves into a course of action that would bring glamour and entertainment for the fans, a rewarding challenge for the players and untold riches financially, but, of course, the dire catastrophe of the Munich air crash was just two years down the line.

It was at this point that a letter arrived from the Football League forbidding United to enter as secretary Alan Hardaker and his management committee feared that the club's entry would undermine their own competition.

United turned to the Football Association for support and found Stanley Rous, the secretary, later to become Sir Stanley, President of FIFA, encouraging United to go ahead. The Football League had also not bargained for the quiet strength of United's doughty, elderly chairman, Harold Hardman, an England amateur player, who won four caps for the full international team and, like Busby, was something of a visionary.

Hardman had played at outside left as an amateur in the Everton team that had won the FA Cup in 1906, and he won an Olympic medal in 1908. Later when he was a director of United, he played for Stoke in the Southern League. Because of his legal background he probably knew that, legally, the club were entitled to pursue this new ambition.

He was on the board altogether for fifty years and a legend in his own right, as he later showed when faced with the carnage of Munich and the football world wondered if the tragedy would wipe out the club as an entity, as well as a famous team. The fact that it didn't owes much to the calm leadership of Harold Hardman in the hour of need and his determination that the club should rise again.

Busby himself had no doubts, as he later explained: 'When I led Manchester United into Europe in 1956, in the face of

League opposition, some people called me a visionary, others a reactionary, while a few thought me just plain awkward and stubborn. Certainly I was eager to be part of this new European challenge. There was money to be made for the club, there was a new kind of adrenalin-inducing excitement for the players and there was the opportunity for the spectators to enjoy the skills of Continental players. It always seemed to me a logical progression that the champions of Europe should pit their abilities against the best of Europe. You cannot make progress standing still.'

Looking back now, United's resolve to enter the European Cup was a significant landmark in the development of English football, and proved to be a decision that would be a key factor in United's emergence as a global power in the game.

Although he didn't quite say as much at the time, Busby also knew that he had gathered around him a band of players quite capable of taking on the big guns of Europe, and it soon became evident that he was not kidding himself.

Their first European tie was away to Anderlecht, the Belgian champions, and United came home from Brussels with a 2–0 win, the goals scored by the all-conquering partnership of Viollet and Taylor. It was a useful scoreline but gave little indication of what was to come in the second leg played at Maine Road (Old Trafford didn't have floodlights).

United romped to a breathtaking 10–0 victory to prompt the comment from Jef Mermans, the Belgian international and opposing captain: 'After United had scored their sixth goal, they still ran as hard as they had done at the start. We have played against the best teams of Hungary and Russia and never been beaten like this. Why don't they pick this team for England?' he asked.

The Welsh referee, Mervyn Griffiths, added: 'I have never seen football more deadly in execution.'

United had lit a fuse of excitement, quickly picked up by their fans who, like all English football followers of the time, had almost become accustomed to the sad decline of our international team. In 1953, they had suffered the indignity of Hungary coming to Wembley and winning 6–3 at the home of football, and then, just to prove it had not been a fluke, they thrashed us 7–1 in Budapest six months later. There had also been the humiliation of losing 1–0 to the United States, when England failed to get past the first-round group stage at the 1950 World Cup.

Now, in contrast, albeit with just a club side, the nation had a team taking on Europe and proving good enough to win.

United knocked out Borussia Dortmund in the next round and then faced Athletic Bilbao in what turned out to be a tie that gripped the public in places far removed from Manchester. The Reds lost the first leg of their quarter-final 5–3 in Spain and seemingly had reached the end of the road. Nobody thought they had a chance in the second leg at Maine Road (they *still* didn't have floodlights at Old Trafford).

The Bilbao manager announced that no team had ever scored three goals against them, but United were inspired, as Viollet and Taylor struck and then in a thrilling climax, Taylor worked an opening for Johnny Berry to put away.

As Henry Rose of the *Daily Express*, the sports writer who had doubted the ability of Taylor, happily conceded in his report: 'My hands are still trembling as I write. My heart still pounds. And a few hours have passed since, with 65,000 other lucky people, I saw the greatest soccer victory in history, ninety minutes of tremendous thrill and excitement that will live for ever in the memory. Salute to the eleven red-shirted heroes of Manchester United. The whole country is proud of you. Hammering in my brain, almost shattering my senses, is the still-fresh memory of the spectacle of eleven brave, gallant footballers battering, pounding until they had them on their knees almost crying for mercy, a team of Spaniards ranked as one of the best club teams in the world.'

The semi-final lined United up against the kings of Europe, mighty Real Madrid, who won the opening leg in the Bernabeu Stadium 3–1 in front of 120,000 people. Bobby Charlton came in for the return leg, staged at Old Trafford following the installation of floodlights, and marked his European debut by scoring in a highly creditable 2–2 draw.

Real went on to beat Fiorentina in the final to remain European champions but United had emerged with credit and as Busby summed up: 'A great, experienced team will always triumph over a great, inexperienced one, but our time will come.'

He could well afford to speak with such confidence as his team took all before them again in the League and were declared champions by Easter, finishing eight points ahead of Spurs. Their scoring topped the century mark: made up of twenty-six by Billy Whelan, twenty-two from Tommy Taylor, sixteen from Dennis Viollet and ten from Bobby Charlton in fourteen appearances following a debut against Charlton Athletic, in which he scored twice in a 4–2 win.

After winning the title, Busby rested a number of players for the FA Cup and played seven reserves against Burnley at Old Trafford. But the Football League were hardly in a position to complain that he hadn't played a full-strength team because the reshaped side won 2–0 with a goal from Alex Dawson on his debut and another from ever-ready reserve Colin Webster.

Then, to further underline their strength in depth, the second team, made up largely of youth team players, won 3–1 on the same day, at Burnley.

The run in the FA Cup had gone well, with Hartlepool, Wrexham, Everton, Bournemouth and Birmingham all dispatched, to take them to Wembley to meet Aston Villa.

I remember Matt Busby telling me years later that, when he came down the stairs of the Cup final hotel on the morning of the match, he had never felt more sure of anything in his life: that Manchester United would win, to give him the prize of a League and Cup double, to compensate for losing out in Europe.

Of course the only certainty in football is its uncertainty and nobody could have foreseen the collision between Ray Wood and Peter McParland just six minutes into the match. The United goalkeeper was carried off with a fractured cheekbone. The Villa striker had headed the ball into Wood's arms but, perhaps fired up for the final, had kept coming and crashed into him.

It was an unfair charge, even allowing for the way that goalkeepers could be challenged in those days, and, of course, this was the era before substitutes were allowed. So United had to reorganise. Jackie Blanchflower took over in goal and the ten men played bravely, to go off at the interval with the score still goalless.

Physiotherapist Ted Dalton took the injured Wood behind the stadium to test him by throwing the ball at him, but as the manager said afterwards: 'Poor Ray saw no more than a couple out of every six balls put to him.'

In the second half Wood was sent on for spells on the right wing, as nuisance value, but Villa sensed they had their opponents at their mercy and, ironically, the villain turned hero as far as Villa were concerned, and McParland rattled in a couple of goals. Tommy Taylor managed to score with a header and in a last desperate bid for victory, Busby put the dazed Wood back into goal so that his outfield could resume their normal shape.

They tried hard, but couldn't force the issue and the dream of a double collapsed.

It had been a courageous effort and once the immediate disappointment had been accepted, Busby was satisfied that his plans were bearing fruit and that with such a young squad at his disposal, they were certainly going to pose a treble threat the following season.

And they started off in fine style, scoring not less than three goals in each of their opening six games, before coming a cropper against Bolton, which triggered a lean spell, with three defeats in four games. They steadied down around Christmas and again moved convincingly through the FA Cup, knocking out Workington and Ipswich while also taking Europe by storm once more.

In Europe, Shamrock Rovers were knocked out and they eased through against Dukla Prague before beating Red Star Belgrade 2–1 at Old Trafford in the first leg of the European Cup quarter-final.

On 1 February they played their final League game before flying out to Belgrade for the return leg. This dramatic 5–4 win against Arsenal at Highbury somehow expressed all the power and panache of the fine young team Matt Busby had created.

It was the last match the Busby Babes played in this country, and certainly a fitting one, before setting off for Belgrade and drawing a tough game 3–3 to ease their way into the semi-finals for the second season running.

Then it was time for the flight home.

Chapter Fifteen

THE WORLD STOPPED

———

Towards tea time at the end of the day in a busy evening newspaper office, the urgency and tensions slacken. The final edition had been put to bed, and on this particular late afternoon of 6 February 1958, the abrupt shouts of 'Boy' matured into polite requests for messengers.

Suddenly, though, as the staff of the *Manchester Evening News* began to think of tea and home, or even a pint to give the traffic time to clear, there was a rushed message from the wire room breaking the news that the plane bringing the Manchester United team home had crashed when trying to take off at Munich after a refuelling stop.

Even though the first reports gave no indication of the dreadful calamity that was to unfold, it was nevertheless a significant story for the team's local paper whose own reporter, Tom Jackson, was with the press party travelling with the team.

The first message said simply that United had been delayed and a paragraph in the Stop Press announced: 'United plane held up in Munich blizzard.'

Then came a more serious flash from the Press Association

and the headline was quickly rushed into the final edition reading: 'Manchester United in plane crash.'

The report said that they were searching for survivors and those of us still in the office were gripped and numbed by the startling news.

Editor Tom Henry, a United fan himself and friend of Matt Busby, quickly appreciated the enormity of what was happening. He gathered together a team of senior reporters and subeditors, sent everyone else home, and got down to producing a special late edition that was printed later that evening.

People had gathered outside the office in Cross Street, where Boots the chemists now stands, to read and discover that Manchester's worst fears were being realised.

The Busby Babes had already won a special place in the affections of the Manchester public. They were young and they had mostly grown up at Old Trafford after being signed straight from school. They played exciting and successful football. They had blazed a trail for English football in European competition and brought the likes of the fabled Real Madrid to the city.

The team had become family and the news hit people like a personal bereavement. They were stunned. For a great many, the world seemed to have stopped and left them in limbo, so close to home was the accident. People spoke quietly on the buses and trains as the drama progressed over the coming days, with twenty-one-year-old Duncan Edwards, a brave heart indeed, fighting vainly over the next two weeks for his life.

The daily bulletins from the Rechts der Isar Hospital in Munich were followed intently.

Vincent Mulchrone of the *Daily Mail* caught the mood of Manchester when he wrote: 'In the past the heart of a community may have been in the church, or the castle, perhaps the local pub. Today there is no doubt that the heart of this city lies with a football team.'

As the writer H E Bates movingly put it as he heard the news on television: 'As the news came on, the screen seemed to go blank. The normally urbane voice of the announcer seemed to turn into a sledgehammer. My eyes went deathly cold and I sat listening with a frozen brain to that cruel and shocking list of casualties.'

Jimmy Murphy heard the news from Matt Busby's secretary. 'Seven of the greatest players ever assembled in one club wiped out, and the greatest of them all, Duncan Edwards, fighting for his life. I was like a man living through a nightmare waiting to wake up. I locked the door, put my head on the desk and wept like a child,' he said.

Nobby Stiles, one of the players too young to make the squad for the trip and who cleaned the boots of the first-teamers, found out what had happened in Munich when he changed buses in the centre of Manchester on his way home from Old Trafford. He bought an *Evening Chronicle* and thought it was strange seeing the faces of Roger Byrne and other team-mates staring out of the front page.

He described it in his book *After the Ball*: 'They belonged at the back of the paper. But they were dead. Eddie Colman was dead. He couldn't be dead. I cleaned his boots. None of them could be dead, but especially not Coly. But that's what the *Chronicle* was saying in big black headlines.

'I felt sick. I got on the Collyhurst bus and I didn't hear anything going on around me. Everything seemed normal enough. The streets and shops looked just the same. The sun was presumably still up there behind the low leaden sky, and

I guessed the moon would take its place in a few hours' time.

'I knew nobody would be at home. I couldn't face an empty house. When I got off the bus I walked across Rochdale Road and down Livesey Street and into the church. I prayed and prayed. Prayed that the *Chronicle* had got it all wrong, had played the sickest practical joke in the history of newspapers. I prayed and I wept. I sat back in the pew for a long time. It could have been an hour or two, I don't really know. There was no one else in the church. Then I went home. The house, as I expected, was empty. The lads were dead, or so I had read, but people still had to work. I put the dinner in the oven.'

People all over Manchester, and farther away as the news spread, also went through the motions of ordinary living, but there was a hush in the city the next day, and for many tears were never far away.

I remember conversation in the train on the way to work the next day was stilted and awkward, like it is in the car on the way to a funeral. The next day's paper was produced without the usual banter that flourishes in a newspaper office.

My mind was focused on the tragedy because I was the leader writer who had to express the paper's sorrow and the grievous blow suffered, it seemed, by everyone, as the tragedy united us in grief.

The next day I was moved nearer to the centre of the story when editor Tom Henry asked me to take over as the United reporter in the absence of Tom Jackson, who had written about the Reds for twenty-five years.

Football itself had taken a back seat of course. The stories were centred on the life and death struggles in the Munich hospital, Jean Busby's visit to see her stricken husband, and then about Jimmy Murphy bringing home the two survivors who had

Fitness training, 1957 style. Duncan Edwards, Johnny Berry, Dennis Viollet, Bill Foulkes, Roger Byrne, Wilf McGuinness, Mark Jones and Billy Whelan get into shape. (*Empics*)

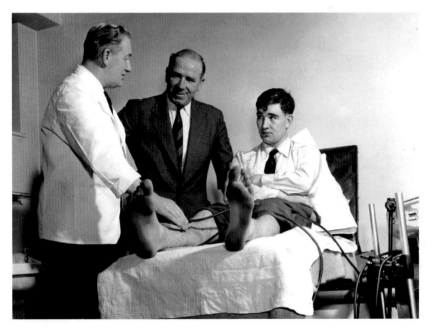

Ted Dalton, the physio, explains an injury to Matt Busby and Jackie Blanchflower. (*Popperfoto*)

Villa's Peter McParland charges into Ray Wood early in the 1957 FA Cup final, a moment that changed the entire balance of the tie and prevented United from securing a famous Double. (*Empics*)

Tommy Taylor falling backwards after scoring United's consolation goal against Villa in their 2–1 defeat. (*Empics*)

Hero to a generation: Duncan Edwards signs an autograph for a fan just before United's game against Arsenal on 1 February 1958 – a scintillating 5–4 victory, it was to be his last game in England. (*Popperfoto*)

The United team boarding their plane to Belgrade on 3 February for their European Cup tie. (*Popperfoto*)

The Busby Babes line up for the last time against Red Star Belgrade. (*Empics*)

The crashed wreckage of the Lord Burleigh plane on the runway. Geoff Bent, Roger Byrne, Eddie Colman, Duncan Edwards, Mark Jones, David Pegg, Tommy Taylor and Billy Whelan were the eight United players to lose their lives in the Munich disaster, along with fifteen others, including club secretary Walter Crickmer, trainer Tom Curry and coach Bert Whalley. (*Empics*)

Munich hero Harry Gregg, assistant manager Jimmy Murphy and Bill Foulkes begin their long journey back to Manchester, the horror of their experience etched on their faces. (*Empics*)

Bill Foulkes leads out a patched up Manchester United side for their fifth round FA Cup tie against Sheffield Wednesday on 19 February. On a night of overwhelming emotion, in front of a crowd of 60,000, United showed they were ready to fight on. (*Empics*)

Nat Lofthouse challenges Harry Gregg during the 1958 FA Cup final, while Stan Crowther looks on. Sadly, United couldn't bring home the trophy in tribute to their fallen team-mates. (*Getty Images*)

The Munich survivors gather in 1997 ahead of the Champions League final: (left to right) Kenny Morgans, Sir Bobby Charlton, Harry Gregg, Jackie Blanchflower, Dennis Viollet, Bill Foulkes, Ray Wood and Albert Scanlon. (*Empics*)

The rebuilding process begins. (Right) Matt Busby, Jimmy Murphy and trainer Jack Crompton plan for the season ahead in August 1961. But it was with the record signing of Denis Law (below) in the summer of 1962 that one of the first key steps to the building of a new great side was made. Denis signs, watched by Gigi Peronace, United's Italian agent, Jimmy Murphy and Matt Busby. (*Empics*)

David Herd, watched by Denis Law, scores the second goal against Leicester's Gordon Banks to help United to a 3–1 victory in the FA Cup final of 1963. Between them they scored 50 goals in the season. (*Getty Images*)

Bobby Charlton, captain Noel Cantwell, Pat Crerand, Albert Quixall and David Herd celebrate United's first trophy in six years. It was the start of another golden period under Busby. (*Popperfoto*)

escaped with hardly a scratch, Harry Gregg and Bill Foulkes.

Then it was the turn of the dead, with people lining the route from the airport to Old Trafford where the bodies were temporarily laid to rest in the gymnasium that had been turned into a morgue.

Then came the funerals and the declaration from Manchester United's sturdy little chairman, Harold Hardman: 'Although we mourn our dead and grieve for our wounded we believe that great days are not done for us. The sympathy and encouragement of the football world and particularly of our supporters will justify and inspire us. The road back may be long and hard but with the memory of those who died at Munich, of their stirring achievements and wonderful sports-manship ever with us, Manchester United will rise again.'

United's scheduled First Division game against Wolves on the Saturday was immediately postponed and they were given a two-week respite before returning to action on 19 February in the fifth round of the FA Cup against Sheffield Wednesday, at Old Trafford. My first stories were about the signing of Ernie Taylor from Blackpool and then the transfer of Stan Crowther for £22,000 completed just an hour before kick-off.

I thought I would never reach Old Trafford on the night of the match, such was the crush of traffic, with as many people leaving as trying to get in, because the ground was so hope-lessly full.

A tide of emotion took United past the luckless Sheffield Wednesday 3–0, with the fans, emotions bottled up for nearly a fortnight, at last able to give vent to their feelings in a way other than grief.

Then, after a 1–1 draw against Nottingham Forest at Old Trafford three days later, Jimmy Murphy decided the playing side needed a break, in order to prepare for the next round of the FA Cup at West Bromwich Albion.

He gathered about him a large squad of players, reaching down to the junior A team, and took them by coach to Blackpool to stay at the Norbreck Hydro Hotel.

The press pack, itself made up of people like me, hurriedly promoted to take the places of our lost colleagues, gathered there for Jimmy Murphy's daily news bulletins.

The players trained nearby but dressed and showered in the swimming pool changing rooms, with Murphy holding his press conferences poolside. I shall forever associate the smell of the baths' chlorine with my early stories about Manchester United after Munich. It was an unreal time, and though people found the matches a release because it was an opportunity to let go and simply roar out encouragement, even the games seemed surreal.

As Shay Brennan, hero of the hour on his debut against Sheffield Wednesday in the Cup tie, recollected: 'Everyone was just lost in his own thoughts in the dressing room. There are always jokers in a football changing room but nobody was laughing or larking about that night.'

Brennan, never a winger, nevertheless played on the left wing and scored two of the goals. Later he admitted to me: 'I remember one of my goals was direct from a corner. It was the first time I had ever taken a corner. My only thought was to put in a decent cross. It was a bad corner, and if it hadn't been for the wind it would have been the 'keeper's ball. I scored another from close in and suddenly, from being plain old Brennan to most people, I was now "Shay".

'Normally I would have gone for a drink after the match. But on that night I just wanted to go home. I'll never forget that so many friends and a great team died to enable that to happen.'

The Busby Babes had celebrated after coming through against Red Star to reach the semi-finals of the European Cup, and why not, they had everything to play for and everything to live for. The football world lay at their feet, but as they boarded their Elizabethan aircraft the next day to head for home and the fateful refuelling stop at Munich, they little knew that where they chose to sit on the plane would largely dictate whether they lived or died.

Those at the rear of the plane, where the press always sit on trips with football teams, all perished because the tail broke off and was engulfed in flames. Eight writers lost their lives. Frank Taylor of the *News Chronicle* was the only survivor, the only journalist to sit further forward. With tragic irony, David Pegg had changed seats between take-offs, saying he was going to sit at the back because he felt it was safer. If he hadn't moved and had stayed with his card school, he might have had a chance.

The United plane landed at Munich as snow was falling, to add to the slush on the ground, and everyone hurried into the terminal building for tea and coffee. The refuelling did not take long though and they were soon back on the plane ready for take-off and the flight home.

The airfield was now covered in snow and all the survivors spoke afterwards about the slush on the runway, which was later found to be the cause of the failure to take off, despite early attempts by a German inquiry to blame ice on the wings.

At 14.19 hours, Captain Ken Rayment, the pilot for the flight, with Captain James Thain, the commander, sitting alongside him, requested permission to taxi out for take-off.

At 14.30 Radio Officer Bill Rodgers told the control tower that 609 Zulu Uniform was rolling and a horrific drama had begun.

Some forty seconds later the plane pulled up. The pilots were concerned that the engines were giving out an uneven note. Power surging was not uncommon with Elizabethans and apparently the pilots were not unduly worried. They requested permission for a second attempt. Another charge down the runway began but again Captain Thain abandoned the take off after thundering half its length. He was not satisfied with the pressure reading from the port engine.

The aircraft returned to the terminal building and the passengers went into the lounge while the pilots conferred with the station engineer, William Black. The question of an overnight stop cropped up, but no one really wanted that kind of inconvenience and everyone trooped out for a third attempt. Alf Clarke, the *Manchester Evening Chronicle* reporter, was nearly left behind because he had been on the phone to his office with the story of the delay. He dashed out just in time and at 14.56 the plane taxied out to the runway. At 15.03 Zulu Uniform started a third attempt to take off and this time there was no pulling up.

Of the forty-three people on board the *Lord Burghley*, twenty-three died either in the crash or soon afterwards. They were:

Players: Roger Byrne, Geoff Bent, Eddie Colman, Mark Jones, David Pegg, Tommy Taylor, Liam (Billy) Whelan, Duncan Edwards (died 21 February).
Officials: Walter Crickmer (secretary), Tom Curry (trainer), Bert Whalley (coach).
Journalists: Alf Clarke (*Evening Chronicle*), Don Davies (*Guardian*), George Follows (*Daily Herald*), Tom Jackson

(*Manchester Evening News*), Archie Ledbrooke (*Daily Mirror*), Henry Rose (*Daily Express*), Frank Swift (*News of the World*), Eric Thompson (*Daily Mail*).

Crew: Captain K G Rayment (co-pilot), Mr W T Cable (steward).

Others: Mr B P Miklos (travel agent), Willie Satinoff (United supporter).

The twenty survivors were:

Players: Johnny Berry, Jackie Blanchflower, Bobby Charlton, Bill Foulkes, Harry Gregg, Kenny Morgans, Albert Scanlon, Dennis Viollet, Ray Wood.

Journalists: Ted Ellyard and Peter Howard (*Daily Mail* photographers), Frank Taylor (*News Chronicle*).

Crew: Captain James Thain (pilot), George Rodgers (radio officer), Margaret Bellis and Rosemary Cheverton (stewardesses).

Others: Mrs Vera Lukic and baby Vesna, Mrs B P Miklos, Mr N Tomasevic.

Chapter Sixteen

DEMONS

———

For years Harry Gregg found it difficult to face his memories of the Munich air crash, the horror of losing so many friends, even ignoring the fact that he went back into the crashed plane, to rescue a baby and her mother.

He finally confronted what he described as his demons on the occasion of the fortieth anniversary of the tragedy that was marked by a charity match at Old Trafford.

Harry ended his long silence in a private box overlooking the Old Trafford pitch when he told me: 'We landed at Munich for a refuelling stop. It was snowing slightly and there were footprints in the snow as we made our way into the terminal. We got back on and there was nothing untoward as we set off down the runway.

'I watched the telescopic leg of the wheel on my side extend as we went towards lift-off. I watched the wheel lock and unlock with the plane swerving about a little bit. Then the aircraft stopped and someone came on to say we would be going back to make another attempt. I just supposed it was a technical hitch.

'We set off again, going a little bit further this time. It was like a speedboat at sea with a bow wave as the snow got deeper. We pulled up again and it was quite unnerving. This time they said we would be going back into the terminal and the party would disembark.

'In less than five minutes we were called back on and we boarded again. I watched the steward belting himself in and I thought it was perhaps more serious than I had realised. So I made a point of getting well down in my seat, undid my collar and tie, and put my feet on the chair in front.

'We started to roll until someone said we were one short. It was Alf Clarke from the *Evening Chronicle*. He came on board and we set off once again. I was reading a book that wasn't too kind to the way I had been brought up so I put it down. I thought if I get killed reading a book like that I'd go to Hell, which was the way of life in those days.

'I kept watching the wheels and I thought we were away this time because we were going past places I had not seen before. I couldn't see the fence because you can't see ahead from inside a plane. I thought we had lifted until all of a sudden there was this horrendous noise. It felt as if everything was upside down, one minute daylight the next darkness, with the awful sound of tearing, ripping, smoke and flames.

'The first thump I got was on the back of the head, then on the front of my head. I felt something going up my nose and I just didn't know what was going on. I had not long joined Manchester United, I was married and had one child, and in my simple mind I thought I had done well for the first time in my life and that I wouldn't see my wife, little girl and parents again. I also worried that I couldn't speak German. Why I thought that I have no idea. Everything seemed to be in slow motion.

'All of a sudden it all stopped. There was nothing but darkness and I thought it must be Hell because of the blackness. I just lay there for a while and felt the blood running down my face. I was afraid to reach up for fear of what I would find.

'Then I realised I couldn't be dead. There was some burning and sparks from wires. Above me to the right was a hole and daylight. I started to crawl towards it and in the darkness went over one or two people. I looked out of the hole and directly below me was Bert Whalley, the team coach, wearing an air force blue suit. His eyes were wide open and he hadn't a mark on him.

'I made the hole bigger and dropped down beside Bert. In the distance I could see five people running through the snow and shouting, "Run, run, it's going to explode." I just stood there. I think the fear factor had gone, I really don't know, but from around what was left of the cockpit came the pilot, Captain Thain, and he also shouted, "Run, you stupid bastard, it's going to explode," and ran back the way he had come.

'Just then I heard a child crying and I shouted, "There are people still alive in here." I crawled back in terrified of what I was going to find. I found the child under a pile of rubbish and crawled out. The radio operator came back and I gave him the child. I went back in and found the mother. She was in a shocking state and I had to literally kick her through the hole to send her on her way.

'I found Ray Wood and was sure he was dead. I couldn't get him out. I saw Albert Scanlon and he looked even worse. I tried to drag him out but he was trapped by the feet and I had to put him down.

'I got out and went round the back of the aircraft where I found Bobby Charlton and Dennis Viollet hanging half in and half out of the stump of the plane. I dragged them clear by the waistbands of their trousers and left them about fifteen yards away.

'I got round the other side and at that point realised how bad it was with the rest of the plane sticking out of what I later learned was a fuel store and it was on fire. Between that and the part of the plane I had come out of was the Boss. He was sitting up on his elbows with his hands across his chest and moaning a terrible "Aargh."

'He had a bad cut behind his ear and one of his feet was bent back the wrong way but he didn't look too bad compared with what I had seen. I thought I could leave him. I put something behind him to support his back and said, "You're OK, Boss."

'I went another twenty yards and found Jackie Blanchflower. The snow was melting around him because of the heat and the burning part of the aircraft. He was crying out that he had broken his back and was paralysed. I looked and saw Roger Byrne lying across him and I don't think Jackie had realised that it was Roger's body which was holding him down.

'Roger didn't have a mark on him. He was a handsome fellow, handsome in life and handsome in death. I kept talking to "Blanchy". His right arm was almost severed and I took my tie off to tie round his arm. I pulled so hard I broke it. I looked up and one of the stewardesses was standing there. I asked her to get something to tie his arm with but the poor girl was in shock, so I just used what was left of my tie.

'I stayed with him until a fellow in a tweed coat turned up with a medical bag and carrying a syringe. There were explosions going on and one made him jump so much he ended up on his backside but still holding the syringe up in the air.

'People came from across the fields, ordinary people, not rescue people. I didn't see any of those at all. Eventually a Volkswagen arrived which was a coal van. Jackie was put into it, also Johnny Berry who I didn't even recognise as a player until I saw the badge on his blazer. Myself, Billy Foulkes and Dennis Viollet were also put in and we were driven to the hospital.

'I remember breaking down and crying when we got there and I saw Bobby Charlton, Peter Howard, Ted Ellyard and a big Yugoslav [a journalist friend of the travel agent travelling with the party]. I was just relieved that there were more of us alive. Some of us were asked to identify people they were working on. Ray Wood was lying on the floor as they attended to his eye.

'They gave us a bowl of soup and the Yugoslav collapsed. He just slid down the wall. He had been walking around with a broken leg which suddenly gave way. They started to give us injections. Bobby fainted and so he was kept in hospital. Billy Foulkes, Ted, Peter and I were taken to a hotel where the people looked after us wonderfully.

'Jimmy Murphy turned up the following day with Jean Busby, Sandy Busby, Duncan's father, Gladstone, Jimmy Payne, Duncan's best friend, Jackie's dad and the wives like Jean Blanchflower.

'Jean Busby at that time was remarkable. She took care of everyone and encouraged the other wives while all the time her own husband was upstairs fighting for his life. She was strong, very, very strong.

'I had to go back to the hospital the next day. I could hardly get out of bed because of my back. They gave me injections to the point where I said, "That's enough," because the injections were worse than the bad back. Jimmy Murphy asked Bill and I to stay for a few days so that those lying in hospital wouldn't realise the full extent of the accident.

'Eventually Professor Maurer took Jimmy, Bill and myself round the wards and would stop at the foot of each bed to tell us their chances of survival. The Boss: fifty–fifty because he was a strong man; Jackie Blanchflower OK; Duncan fifty–fifty; but when he got to little Johnny Berry he whispered, "No, no, I am not God." Johnny survived of course but unhappily died a few years ago, like some of the others.

'Duncan Edwards woke up when we went into his room and he asked us: "What time is kick-off?" Quick as a flash Jimmy Murphy told him, "Three o'clock, son." Duncan responded: "Get stuck in."

'Bill and I came home and I remember about ten days afterwards all the newspapers in my house kept disappearing. I couldn't figure out what was going on until I realised they were being hidden from me. Big Duncan had died. I found that hard. It hit me terribly. Yes, that was Munich.

'A lot of people wondered where Matt Busby got the strength from to return to football and start all over again. I went to see him shortly after he got back to England. He had aged terribly and he told me that the hardest part for him after the crash was the way Johnny Berry kept coming to his room to say: "Tommy Taylor's some friend of mine, he hasn't even been to see me." Johnny didn't know the full extent of the crash and Matt said he just didn't know what to say to him.

'He told me: "Son, they couldn't give me an anaesthetic to set my broken foot because of my chest injuries, so they set it a bone at a time, one every day. It was cruel, but it didn't hurt me like Johnny Berry coming into my room every day to say Tommy Taylor was a poor friend."

'It was awful for Jimmy [Murphy] after the crash, too. He had so much to do. I remember in Munich walking up the stairs to my room and I was one flight from the top when I heard this terrible crying. At first I couldn't figure it out but as I got nearer I could just make out Jimmy sitting in the dark on the empty staircase crying his eyes out. I just quietly walked away.

'Matt and Jimmy were oil and water as people but they were a wonderful partnership. I believe the greatness of Manchester United was founded on their strength and friendship, but after Munich it was the strength of Matt's wife, Jean, which enabled Matt to return and rebuild the shattered club.'

Harry Gregg was certainly the stuff of legend at Munich and I believe his heroic action going back into the plane deserves more recognition than he has received; indeed I was contacted some years afterwards by someone who was petitioning for the Irishman to be awarded a medal, but without success. Perhaps it was because it wasn't until years afterwards that the full facts of Munich became known, and not least because the man himself chose to stay silent for forty years on the part he had played.

Busby signed Harry two months before the crash, after a mid-season blip. Perhaps significantly, after making his debut in a 4–0 home win against Leicester, the League results immediately began to improve.

Later, his boots were cleaned by George Best, for whom he remained an idol and a hero throughout his life, as George explained: 'I considered it an honour to be given the task of cleaning his boots; such were the chores of an apprentice in those days. He really was respected and loved at the club. Not only had he survived the Munich air crash in which so many of his team-mates and friends had perished, but he had bravely gone back into the burning wreckage of the aeroplane to rescue a young woman, her baby and others. As I got older and talked to various people still at the club who were there that fateful day, the enormity of Harry's actions sunk in and he continued to rise in my estimation. Bravery is one thing – all goalkeepers must have it to a certain degree – but what Harry did that day was about more than bravery. It was about goodness.

'I first met Harry on the training ground in 1961 when I was a wisp of a lad arriving at Manchester United for the first time. It was my greatest thrill to meet him in the flesh, as back in Northern Ireland he was the player revered by all fans more than any other, no mean feat for a goalkeeper. One reason was because he had been part of the most successful national football side in Irish history when they battled through to the last eight of the 1958 World Cup finals – FIFA voted him the best goalkeeper at the tournament – and the other because he kept goal for Manchester United, the English club supported by more Irish people than any other.

'Sir Matt Busby pushed us together straight away because he thought that Harry would be a steadying and parental influence on me and perhaps banish any thoughts I might have had of disappearing back to the comfort of my family, home and friends in Belfast.

'I was struck by the sheer size of him but he put me at ease immediately with his kindness and gentle manner.'

Finally, in a handsome foreword to Gregg's autobiography *Harry's Game*, George said: 'I know Harry, like my father, was worried during my darkest days but, like my Dad, he would never have presumed to tell me how to live my life. Harry

Gregg was a great athlete and a great man. Harry, you're my hero – and I mean that.'

Harry certainly played the part as George Best's mentor, even persuading Bertie Peacock to give him his debut for Northern Ireland without 'the manager' actually having seen him play.

Amazingly, with hardly a scratch on him, Harry came back to Manchester after Munich with the similarly unscathed Bill Foulkes, to play a key role in the recovery of the club and provide a link with the next era. He was literally a tower of strength in the FA Cup run to the final, but his runner-up medal was his only honour before a shoulder injury handicapped him and prompted a reluctant transfer to Stoke City in 1966.

He went on to manage Shrewsbury Town, Swansea City and Crewe before returning to Old Trafford to work for Dave Sexton as a youth coach. Harry lost his job with the arrival of Ron Atkinson as manager, and after returning to Swansea as coach and management jobs at Swindon and Carlisle he retired to Northern Ireland to run a hotel. He is retired now, living by the sea, walking the beaches on the coast of Londonderry and perhaps contemplating the second great escape of his life – surviving a double whammy of bowel and prostate cancer.

Chapter Seventeen

KEEP THE FLAG
FLYING

═══

Jimmy Murphy could hardly hear the words as Matt Busby, fighting for his life in an oxygen tent in Munich, whispered: 'Keep the flag flying, Jimmy.'

United's assistant manager and Matt's right-hand man knew only too well that, with so many dead and stricken following the crash, it now fell to him to do his best to bring some order out of chaos and hopefully enable Manchester United to carry on as a football club.

It was some task. Where to begin and how to find the will to carry on after such a mind-numbing tragedy? How to put back together a club shattered beyond belief?

Fortunately, Manchester United had a legend in the making as Jimmy Murphy stoically and patiently got United functioning as a football club again. Without Jimmy Murphy, it is possible that the Old Trafford club might have collapsed and sunk out of sight. Even before Munich, he had contributed far more than was appreciated outside Old Trafford, playing a key role behind the scenes in the transformation of a sleeping giant to the point where the Busby Babes were sweeping all before them.

Munich thrust Murphy for once into the full glare of the spotlight, so much so that he could have become manager of Juventus if he had been prepared to leave United.

Juventus had been impressed by the way he had held Old Trafford together during the chaos that inevitably followed the disaster while Sir Matt Busby was battling for his life in hospital. The Italians had also admired the way that, as the manager of Wales, he had taken the mixed bag of players who made up his team to the quarter-finals of the 1958 World Cup in Sweden.

The 'Old Lady' used John Charles, the Welsh international who played for the Italian giants at the time, as their intermediary and authorised him to offer Jimmy £20,000 on their behalf. Talking about his attempt to lure Jimmy to Italy, John says: 'He was being offered what was a fortune in those days but he wasn't interested and turned Juventus down.'

Jimmy explained to him: 'I have got to help Matt pick up the pieces and start all over again, we have to rebuild after losing ten players at Munich. Besides, John, how can you put a price on loyalty?'

So Jimmy Murphy stayed with United for the rest of his career and along the way won countless admirers for developing the young players at Old Trafford, both before and after the crash.

Ask any of the Busby Babe survivors or the stars of the sixties and they would tell you how indebted they feel to Jimmy Murphy.

Sir Matt Busby's assistant concentrated on the youngsters, and though it was the manager who lent his name to the famous Babes, it was Murphy who coached and cajoled them on the their way through the junior ranks.

Bobby Charlton, Wilf McGuinness and Nobby Stiles are among the stars who will readily tell you how much they owe to the man who guided their first faltering steps on their way to becoming fully fledged professionals.

Nobby is unstinting in his appreciation of what Murphy taught him. 'I have him to thank for making me into the player I became,' he says. 'Jimmy was the main reason why from the 1940s through to the 1960s Manchester United produced so many world-class players who later became legends. He was a tireless worker, out on the training field morning, noon and night. Next to his family, his only other interest and love was Manchester United.'

Jimmy made an immediate impact on the youthful new recruit from Collyhurst and on his first day at Old Trafford told him: 'This, son,' he said with his arm round his shoulder and full of enthusiasm, 'is the greatest club in the whole world and when you pull on that famous red jersey and run out of this tunnel on to that pitch, you'll feel a special sensation in your whole body, there is no other thrill like it.

'You'll be happy here and we want you to enjoy it with all your heart and soul. Nobby, son, you'll never regret joining us – there is no other club in the world like us.'

On another occasion after a hard training session he told a group of the newcomers: 'This is the place to be, lads, you'll all get a chance here. Show me you can play and before you know it you will be playing in the first team.'

As Nobby says: 'We kids used to like hearing Jimmy saying things like that because it encouraged us. He was the heartbeat of the club. He is an unsung hero and I hope United supporters realise exactly who Jimmy Murphy was and his great contribution to the club. He was one of the greatest teachers and characters it has been my good fortune to have been associated with.'

Bobby Charlton believes he might not have made it to the top without the toughening-up process of going through Murphy's mangle on the training pitch.

'When we played in practice matches he used to come up behind me and kick me. I used to think, "What's going on here?" I couldn't always understand what he was trying to do but now of course I realise he was teaching me what to expect from the harsher side of professional football.

'Jimmy was so intense he used to frighten me. He was hell to work for but everything was done for a purpose and I owe more to Jimmy Murphy than to any other single person in football. I shall always be grateful to him and the success of Manchester United, over so many years, was a testimony to his work.'

Wilf McGuinness, another of Murphy's favourites from the sixties, agrees: 'Without him a lot of us would never have made it as professional footballers. At times we almost hated him because he drove us so hard but it was always for our own good and we certainly respected him.'

Jimmy was a Desert Rat during the war, serving with the Royal Artillery and going through the North African campaign, before arriving at Bari transit camp in Italy, where he took over from Stan Cullis as the sergeant in charge of sport and where he met Matt Busby.

The son of a Welsh mother and Irish father, he was brought up in a little village called Pentre in the Rhondda Valley and as a young man, when he wasn't playing football, he could often be found playing the organ in Treorchy Parish Church.

He played for Wales Schoolboys and when he helped beat England 3–2 at Cardiff and draw 2–2 with Scotland at Hampden Park he came to the attention of English League clubs. He joined West Bromwich Albion, where he played from 1928 until the outbreak of the war, which ended his playing career. He was the youngest player in the Welsh team of his day at the age of twenty-one and in all he was capped twenty-two times as well as captaining his country.

When he teamed up with Busby at the end of the war he said: 'Old Trafford was bombed out and was little more than a rubbish dump. The club just didn't have any money either. We used to give the team their lunch on a match day; only it was across the bridge in an old wooden hut called the United Cafe. They used to get a poached egg.

'As we progressed we started to have lunch at the Trafford Hotel and the food went up the social scale as well, with perhaps boiled chicken on the menu. Later we moved to Gorse Hill and really went up in the world with lamb cutlets, even a steak, but it still wasn't like eating in the Old Trafford Executive Suite!'

Murphy was Busby's first and best signing as Matt freely acknowledged in later years: 'I saw Jimmy Murphy talking football to a crowd of players when we were both in the Army during the war in Italy and I decided then that if ever I needed someone to help me in management, he was my man. We had a wonderful and happy relationship. He was never a yes man, which was a good start and our natures seemed to join to produce commonsense. He was straight, honest and loyal.'

They were totally different people, even as players. Both were wing halves after failing as forwards, but that was where the similarity ended because, while Matt was the gentle giant, his right-hand man was the archetypal Welsh dragon breathing fire and fury. Perhaps the choice of Jimmy as his lieutenant was an acknowledgement by Matt of the lack of aggression in his own make-up.

His team talks were legend and watching from a distance it seemed he was conducting some Welsh choir with his arms and hands punctuating the air to emphasise the effort needed for victory. It was undoubtedly his skill as a motivator that took little Wales through to the quarter-finals of the World Cup where they lost narrowly 1–0 to Brazil, the ultimate winners of the tournament. It was a run that has never been bettered, nor is likely to be.

Sometimes he was not too fussy how he motivated his teams. His players tell of one Welsh game against Germany, in a friendly after the war, when he delivered the usual talk on tactics and wished them luck. Then just as they were about to walk out of the dressing room he called after them: 'And don't forget it was Germans shooting at your fathers not so long ago!'

Looking for players and developing the youngsters in the reserves was Jimmy Murphy's special responsibility and he was the key element in the emergence of the Busby Babes, so that when the crash came, it hit him particularly hard. They were his boys and as he was always fond of saying, he had watched these little apples grow. He also used to tell you that the sun was always shining ... and if you couldn't actually see it, he would explain that it would still be shining behind the clouds! Even Jimmy must have wondered, though, whether the sunshine would ever return to warm his soul.

United's assistant manager had missed the trip to Belgrade to steer Wales through to a World Cup group qualifying win against Israel in Cardiff.

News of the crash was given to him by Alma George, the manager's secretary, on his arrival back at Old Trafford. He was greeted with the terrifying message as he hurried to his office to prepare for the team's arrival: 'The United plane has crashed at Munich.'

Murphy recounts his reaction in his book *Matt ... United ... and Me* with the words: 'My feet stopped. So did my heart. The fingers of the clock on the wall pointed to four o'clock ... but time now meant nothing. The numbing horror of that moment will live with me till I die. I dashed into my office and picked up the phone.'

The weight of the burden handed to Murphy that day must have seemed intolerable. For here was a man overwhelmed with anguish for friends and many of his beloved players, killed, dying or suffering injuries that would end their careers.

Simply to absorb such an experience was emotionally draining, but to be charged also with restoring order out of such chaos and keep Manchester United playing football was a frightful challenge. The hurdles ahead were enormous because not only was there the League programme to complete, United were still in the FA Cup and they were through to the semi-finals of the European Cup, with a daunting draw against AC Milan on the horizon.

The fact that United battled on to finish a respectable ninth in the First Division, reach Wembley to play Bolton in the final and give the Italians two fair games, including a 2–1 victory in the first leg at Old Trafford, says it all for Jimmy Murphy.

Always a shy, retiring man as far as the public were concerned, he rose to the occasion to reveal a strength of character and wisdom that had been somewhat hidden by his role as number two to the much more outgoing and genial Matt Busby.

But cometh the hour, cometh the man and the Welshman who had perhaps been rather taken for granted made sure that Manchester United not only survived, but did so with pride and a surprising success.

The grand European adventure had exacted a terrible price but Murphy had a staunch ally at the club, a tough little old man, too frail to have gone on the trip himself, but resilient and clear thinking. Harold Hardman was also determined that the club would survive and he told Murphy: 'You have got to keep it going Jimmy. Manchester United is bigger than you, bigger than me, bigger than Matt Busby. It is bigger than anybody. The club must go on.'

They were noble words, but where was Murphy to start, just who was there left capable of playing for Manchester United?

Murphy hurried back to Manchester after Busby's whispered plea to keep the flag flying, heartbroken and empty. He did not know whether he would see Busby alive again and he was fearful for the dying Duncan Edwards, the player he well nigh worshipped. As the *Rhinegold Express* thundered out of Bavaria, Murphy says he sat numb while the wheels of the train drummed into his tired brain: 'Where do you find the players? Where do you find the players?'

With him were two of the survivors, goalkeeper Harry Gregg and defender Bill Foulkes. They had escaped the destruction uninjured, though nobody was sure they wouldn't suddenly collapse from delayed shock. They went home to join their families, to leave Jimmy wrestling with the problem of trying to raise a team good enough to represent Manchester United. A squad of seventeen players had flown to Belgrade. Seven had been killed outright, Duncan Edwards was dying, Jackie Blanchflower and Johnny Berry had been so badly injured they wouldn't play again and another five were still in hospital. That left Gregg and Foulkes as the only players from the squad immediately available.

The crash happened on a Thursday. The League fixture on the Saturday at home to Wolves was quickly postponed while their FA Cup fifth round tie against Sheffield Wednesday due the following Saturday was delayed until the Wednesday. It was a welcome breathing space.

Murphy described his task: 'To start with I was in a mental turmoil through sheer sorrow. I also felt completely on my own. Not only was Matt not there, but my great friend, Bert Whalley our coach, had been killed and so had Tom Curry the trainer. I was going to funerals and at the same time trying to sort out what to do.

'My first move was to call on Joe Armstrong, our chief scout and an old faithful, to draw up a complete list of our remaining players. When I looked down the list at those left I groaned. It read like a team of schoolboys. There was plenty of promising talent that might, and indeed did, show itself in two or three years' time, but I needed people immediately.

'I had plenty of letters expressing sympathy from other clubs but I had to learn the hard way that practical help was another matter.'

Only two clubs promised players, Liverpool and Nottingham Forest, but Murphy refused to panic and just take anyone. He didn't want to complicate the future, because he knew their own injured players would return to action, eventually. For a time he contemplated trying to sign Ferenc Puskas, the 'Galloping Major' from Hungary who had starred against them for Real Madrid, but decided it flew in the face of their conviction to make their own players. He decided that at the end of the day, it had to be British players and British guts which would see them through.

Murphy was undoubtedly the inspiration of the Manchester United phoenix which rose after Munich and as Matt Busby said about his partner: 'We worked together to bring greatness to Manchester United and no one outside the club will ever know how important he was to our success. Jimmy Murphy ... the best friend, helper, companion and right-hand man any manager could wish for in this great but risky business of football management.'

Jimmy retired from front-line management when Matt did in 1971, but life without his beloved club was empty and he went back to use his great knowledge scouting for them. On 14 November 1989, just four days after representing United at a match, he collapsed and died as he walked in a park near his home. He was seventy-nine.

Chapter Eighteen

A LIFETIME

Jimmy Murphy was not alone in having to shoulder new responsibilities in terms of finding a team worthy of representing Manchester United after the crash. Others had to step forward, because the administrative side had also been decimated with the death of Walter Crickmer, the secretary who knew the club inside out after long service that included acting as manager during the war. There was nothing Walter didn't know about United. Then, dramatically, his young assistant Les Olive had to take centre stage.

Les had joined United as a boy after writing in for a trial and being accepted as the office boy, with the promise of a game on Saturdays. He answered the telephone, opened the post, weeded the dreaded plantains out of the pitch and mowed the grass, if he could get the machine to work.

He enjoyed his football, too, playing in every position except outside left, for the A and B teams and occasionally the reserves.

After a break of nearly three years' National Service in the RAF, he returned to Old Trafford to be presented with a choice.

He had to decide between playing and concentrating on a career in the office helping secretary Walter Crickmer.

He settled for the office, but continued to play at weekends and was ready to answer an injury crisis. In April 1953 he stepped up to play two games for the first team – as the goalkeeper! He made his debut on the day Dennis Viollet made his bow in the First Division, and together they shared in a 2–1 win at Newcastle, thanks to saving from Bobby Mitchell in a one-on-one situation. He kept his place for a 2–2 draw at home to West Bromwich Albion the following week, before Jack Crompton stepped back into the side.

So now you know the answer to the question: which Manchester United goalkeeper never played on the losing side in a First Division game?

In 1955 he was formally appointed assistant secretary and within three years had to answer another kind of emergency and become acting secretary in place of Walter Crickmer. He was immediately caught up in the maelstrom of emotions and work that was the Munich disaster.

'There was so much to do there was no time to stop and think about the enormity of what had happened, which was perhaps a good thing. People rallied round, especially Alma George, Walter's secretary, and Betty my wife, who as a shorthand typist was of immense help. We sent our daughter, Susan, who was three at the time, to stay with friends and Betty and I worked together fifteen or sixteen hours a day for several weeks. Some of the players were not on the phone and Betty went round to their houses to break the terrible news to their families. The Ground Committee came in to help with the sacks of mail and Freddie Owen, later to become assistant secretary, took a lot on his shoulders as well. Somehow we got through.'

Eventually the club settled down, and Les was officially made secretary. But great changes were on their way under new chairman Louis Edwards, as United headed for their first trophy after Munich – by winning the FA Cup in 1963 – and their other epic achievements in the sixties.

Throughout, even though managers came and went following Busby's retirement, there was always the stability and efficiency of the secretary's department. Les Olive is now a director of Manchester United after an association with the club lasting over sixty years. From tea boy to director, from player to secretary, from mowing the pitch to establishing a reputation as one of the ablest administrators in football, Les Olive has now completed literally a lifetime at Old Trafford.

But he never allowed himself to get carried away. It was even his habit, as secretary, on the morning of every home match to inspect the toilets to make sure they all flushed, and he never lost his zeal for football in the community, long before that phrase was coined.

He has represented United on Manchester County FA since 1959 and is in fact now their honorary president.

He took great change in his stride. Does the big money earned by present-day stars disturb him?

'No, it's the way the game has progressed. The money has been there and you cannot blame the players.'

Did the change of United to a plc trouble him?

'The club had reached the stage where there were two choices, either going public or becoming owned by one man, and I thought the plc move was the safest of the two. Now we are owned by one man again but you have to adapt.

'Manchester United have certainly come a long way in my association of sixty years. When I first joined the club I had a key to every door and room at Old Trafford that I could easily carry on one ring. I think if the secretary attempted to carry all the keys today he would need a wheelbarrow.'

United has certainly come a long way since 1878, when railway workers at the Newton Heath depot, on the fringes of Manchester, got together to form a football team. These days, Old Trafford radiates wealth and power that has left the little, amateurish family football club far behind ... or has it?

Scratch the corporate surface and it's still possible to find a more homely thread running through the organisation. Secretary Ken Merrett has worked at Old Trafford since he was a boy, similarly Ken Ramsden, his assistant, whose mother spent her working life at Old Trafford in the laundry, where she and her colleague were affectionately known as 'Omo and Daz'.

Les worked with seven managers during his time as secretary of Manchester United. Starting with Sir Matt Busby and finishing with Sir Alex Ferguson, he also worked alongside Wilf McGuinness, Frank O'Farrell, Tommy Docherty, Dave Sexton and Ron Atkinson.

'I tried to support all of them to the best of my ability. Perhaps coming from a playing background I could understand their needs and appreciate what was required from my side. I got on well with all of them. I suppose it is my temperament just to get on with things.'

His challenge after the crash, in addition to dealing with families and funerals, was to work closely with Jimmy Murphy on bringing in reinforcements. United made just two immediate ventures into the transfer market. Ernie Taylor was unsettled at Blackpool and wanted to move back to his native northeast, but with the help of Cromford Club owner Paddy

McGrath, a friend of Busby's, Taylor agreed to answer the SOS. He was thirty-one, took only size four in boots, but had been a key man in Newcastle United's FA Cup final victory in 1951 and had schemed Blackpool to their Wembley triumph two years later in the 'Stanley Matthews final' against Bolton.

Murphy paid £8,000 for him and then looked round for a harder man to balance the midfield. He remembered Stan Crowther playing against them for Aston Villa in the previous season's final at Wembley and doing equally well in that season's League fixture at Old Trafford. The hard-tackling Crowther cost £24,000, but importantly, he was granted special permission to play for United in the FA Cup after appearing for Villa in a third round defeat against Stoke City. The deal was rushed through, but the dispensation for him to play against Sheffield Wednesday was not granted by the FA until the afternoon of the match.

The team had the two uninjured survivors in the emergency line-up, Gregg in goal, and Foulkes in his normal right back role. Ian Greaves, who had a little first-team experience, was a natural at left back. Another reserve, Freddie Goodwin, who like Greaves went on to a career in senior management, was picked at wing half with the newly signed Crowther on the other flank.

Colin Webster, a Welsh international, and Taylor were up front but there were still four more places to fill. Murphy called up Ronnie Cope from the A team to play centre half and selected three other unknown teenagers for the remaining places. Mark Pearson, small but sturdy from the Sheffield area, was brought in at inside forward; Alex Dawson, a brawny centre forward who was powerful in the air, was to lead the attack; while a slightly built fullback with an Irish background from

Manchester, Shay Brennan, was put on the left wing to make up the numbers.

In fact Boy Brennan, a dark-haired stripling, emerged the hero in that first match after Munich, scoring twice in a 3–0 win as Sheffield Wednesday faced a tide of emotion as well as a patched-up football team.

Bill Foulkes, promoted to captain in place of Roger Byrne, described the occasion: 'I felt very sorry for Sheffield Wednesday. They were never in the game with a chance, for I'm sure that everyone who took an interest in football, and even those who didn't, were willing us to win that night.'

There was certainly an extraordinary atmosphere, frightening in its intensity, with the poignancy of the occasion illustrated by the match programme, which had been unable to print the line-up of the United team in advance. Underneath the numbers were lines of dots, where the crowd could write in the names themselves, when the team was announced over the loudspeakers. The team lined up was: Gregg, Foulkes, Greaves, Goodwin, Cope, Crowther, Webster, Taylor, Dawson, Pearson, Brennan. 'Murphy's Marvels' went on to draw 2–2 at West Bromwich in the next round before Colin Webster scored for a 1–0 win in the replay.

The semi-final at Villa Park saw Bobby Charlton return to the team in favour of his pal, Brennan, and he scored both goals in a 2–2 draw. Murphy brought Brennan back for the replay at Highbury and this time left out Pearson to make room for Charlton in a thrilling, high-scoring match.

Alex Dawson scored a hat trick with other goals from Charlton and Brennan in a 5–3 victory which took them to Wembley and an all-Lancashire final against near neighbours Bolton.

Dennis Viollet, recovered from his head injuries, was back in time for this one and on paper the team looked its strongest since the crash, but it was as if the tide of emotion had exhausted itself and, of course, Bolton had their own agenda. A fortnight before Munich, United had beaten Bolton 7–2 in the League, but as their rugged England centre forward, Nat Lofthouse, put it: 'All that mattered from our point of view was that Bolton should win the FA Cup.'

Matt Busby was at Wembley but only with the help of walking sticks and Jimmy Murphy led out the team. Lofthouse scored twice in a 2–0 win, his second the result of charging Gregg in the middle of the back and knocking the ball and player into the back of the net, but in truth United were never really in it.

Even reaching Wembley had been a miracle and the point had been well made that United had survived the greatest misfortune ever to befall an English football team, and that survival was testimony to the inspired leadership and superb organisation of Jimmy Murphy.

Chapter Nineteen

TOUGH AND DEPENDABLE

Jimmy Murphy knew he could count on the two players he had brought home from Munich with him. Ignoring the possibility of them suffering a backlash of reaction following their traumatic experience, the names of Harry Gregg and Bill Foulkes were the first he wrote on his team-sheets. They were also a heart-warming presence because not only were they experienced footballers of great ability, they were tough, dependable and ready for what everyone knew would be an uphill struggle.

Bill Foulkes in particular represented the ethos of Manchester United, a founder member of the Busby Babes, who would prove to be the cornerstone of the recovery and a link with the generation of the sixties. For me, this strapping one-time miner became the symbol of the rebuilding because not only had he been in the crash himself; he had the strength of mind needed for the club to survive those traumatic times.

One of my most vivid memories of those early days after the disaster was the crunching matches between Bill and Bolton's equally tough Wyn Davies, as the two players slammed into each other without a flicker of reaction.

I still wince when I think of rock colliding with hard place, with neither player willing to concede that the other guy might have hurt him. No rolling around looking for a free kick from those two.

Bill didn't really know his own strength. Boarding the team bus as the local *Evening News* reporter bound for an away match, it was his habit, by way of a friendly greeting, to punch me on the arm. I was then expected to smile good morning back and make my way to my seat trying to stop my eyes watering. I am happy to say that now we have both reached our three score and ten, he has settled for a more conventional greeting.

Bill always got good marks from me in my reports because, like Sir Matt Busby, who picked him for his first team nearly 700 times, I appreciated the solidity and consistency of his football, no frills, not much finesse, but resolute to the core. Other players tend to be more impressed by the tricky guys in the team and one of them, puzzled by the high marks, once asked me if it was true that he was my brother-in-law. The answer, of course, was no. Neither did the punching influence me; well, not a lot anyway.

I was certainly happy to give him my old bag of golf clubs when he decided to take up the game. They hadn't worked for me and as if to demonstrate that it wasn't the fault of the clubs, Bill took to golf with the same sense of purpose he always brought to his football and he quickly became a scratch golfer. When Bill put his mind to something he made a huge success of it.

Even in the gilded history of Manchester United, few men have loomed larger or lasted longer than Big Bill Foulkes, a legend of longevity.

He checked in at Old Trafford as a seventeen-year old in 1949, the rawest of rookie footballers and still a part-time mineworker, and departed some quarter of a century later, having survived the Munich air disaster, with a glittering array of achievements to his name.

Bill scaled his loftiest pinnacle in the twilight of his playing days, wielding colossal influence as United became the first English club to lift the European Cup in 1968. Before that there had been the little matter of four League Championships – an Old Trafford record until the arrival of the Alex Ferguson era – as well as an FA Cup triumph and an England cap. All the while, the combative Lancastrian was assembling a tally of 682 United appearances, a total that still outstrips all but that of his long-time colleague, Sir Bobby Charlton.

For the better part of two decades Bill was an implacable cornerstone of the Red Devils' rearguard, initially as an efficient right back with the first wave of Busby Babes, then as a towering presence in central defence. Even after all that, the name of Foulkes remained on the club's books, serving four years as a youth coach under Wilf McGuinness, Frank O'Farrell and finally Tommy Docherty. Then, in 1974, Liverpool legend Bob Paisley recommended him for a job in America and he crossed the Atlantic.

It all began when Bill emerged from the rugby stronghold of St Helens, his home town, to enlist with United, in the process disappointing Bolton Wanderers, then a major power in the land and renowned for their muscular defensive methods.

Though playing football part-time – he retained his mining job because he made more money from the pit than from the game – the newcomer progressed steadily at Old Trafford. But, despite a natural self-confidence, there were moments when he wondered if he was in the right place.

'I remember I was growing up with one of the most talented collections of young footballers ever assembled, the Busby Babes. I was strong and willing to work hard, but I would look at the natural ability of some of the others and I'd think I had no chance against them. I never understood why the manager persevered with me, but he must have seen something he liked!'

Indeed, he did, but Bill needed to tell a tiny white lie to his manager in order to secure his senior debut in December 1952. He recalls with a wry grin: 'I was recovering from a sore ankle when our coach, Bert Whalley, told me that Matt wanted to see me in his office. I was petrified because I'd not been able to make the team and I thought I was about to get the old heave-ho. But the Boss was cheerful and said: "Let me see you jump." So I leapt in the air in front of his desk and didn't show the pain I felt when I landed. I told him it was great. He said he was delighted because he was thinking of playing me at right back on Saturday. I thought he meant in the reserves and I was flabbergasted when he told me to travel straight to Anfield from my home in St Helens for the First Division game against Liverpool.'

Bill could hardly have faced a more searching examination, because his direct opponent was the fabulously talented Scottish international Billy Liddell. Understandably, in the circumstances, the youngster was a tad nervous, and nearly half a century later he remains grateful to the Liverpool star for putting him at his ease before kick-off.

'He knew it was my first match and he was a real gentleman. He introduced himself and wished me well. After that, of course, he ran me into the ground as it was his job to do, but there wasn't an ounce of malice in him.'

Bill's recollection of the day is characteristically modest. Although Liddell escaped his marker to put the Merseysiders ahead after ten minutes, United fought back to win and Matt Busby was sufficiently impressed by the right back's gritty display to retain him for the next game at Chelsea.

By then, though, the dodgy ankle was hugely swollen. 'I had to finish the match as a passenger at centre forward, though I did manage to hit the bar with a shot from twenty-five yards. We scored from the rebound and won 3–2, but my ankle was so bad that I didn't play again that season.'

However, Bill was not to be out of the frame for long. During 1953–54 he succeeded veteran John Aston as the regular occupant of United's number two shirt and in October 1954, while still a part-timer, his steady form was rewarded with what was to prove his sole England cap.

He remembers: 'At the time it was a thrill and an honour to be called up against Northern Ireland in Belfast, even if it was only a day after I had worked a shift at the pit! But looking back, I think I played before I was ready for the international stage, and not in what proved to be my best position. I think I might have done myself more justice as a centre half in later years.'

Unfortunately, that call was never to come and in any case, the emergence of Birmingham City's Jeff Hall – who was to lose his life to polio at a tragically tender age – precluded further international advancement at right back.

Still, there was ample compensation at club level for Bill, who consolidated his berth in Matt Busby's scintillating new side and soon had medals to show for it, as the Busby Babes cut loose.

Apart from a short spell towards the end of 1955–56, when he was stretched by National Service commitments and the manager brought in Ian Greaves, Bill was a constant factor in the success of that era, which included of course the first forays into senior European competition by an English club. He recalls with particular clarity the two semi-final meetings with Real Madrid, the majestic Spanish holders of the European crown, in 1957.

'For the players it was a great adventure, a step into the unknown, because although Matt had seen Real play, we knew next to nothing about them. Of course, they were a magnificent team, and he had decided that the less we knew the better! In the first leg at the Bernabeu there were 135,000 people and the noise was incredible. We held our own in the first half but in the second we were undone by Alfredo di Stefano, who played with a number nine on his back but in a deep-lying position from which he could dictate proceedings. In England we were used to playing at one speed and that was 100 mph. But he would change the pace constantly, slowing to a walk, then deliver a sudden clever pass that would enable the left winger, Francisco Gento, to use his explosive pace. At right back I was in direct opposition to Gento, and it was not an easy ride.'

Real took command of the tie, winning 5–3 on aggregate, but United had displayed such verve and spirit of their own that most contemporary pundits reckoned European glory was certain to follow for Busby's precocious young team.

Tragically it didn't come to pass as the Munich disaster intervened. Bill survived, physically unscathed, but carrying untold, unseen hurt that would haunt him for ever. 'How we got through the aftermath of the crash I'll never know. I was made skipper, and somehow we reached Wembley, where we lost to Bolton. Obviously it was a deeply emotional time and the stress caused me to lose weight and, after a while, my form began to slip, too,' he said.

For all that, Bill played a valiant part in a patchwork United's astonishing achievement of finishing as title runners-up to Wolves in season 1958–59, the first full campaign after the tragedy. After a brief break from senior action, he returned to take on the centre half role in the autumn of 1960, quickly emerging as one of the most dominant stoppers in the English game.

Over subsequent seasons Bill proved the trustiest of defensive bulwarks, as Matt moulded his third great United team, acquiring the likes of David Herd, Denis Law and Paddy Crerand, and returned to the trophy trail. In 1963, after a worrying brush with relegation, the FA Cup was garnered and then came League Championships in 1965 and 1967. Bill was an integral part of all that and then, most magical of all, came the European Cup.

Bill was thirty-six by then and suffering from knee problems, but still he was mightily effective alongside Nobby Stiles at the core of the Reds' defence. However, despite his commanding performances at the back, it is for one of his rare goals that Bill's part in that memorable campaign is most frequently recalled. The setting echoed the past in that it was another semi-final against Real Madrid at the Bernabeu. This time, though, it was the second leg and United had come from behind to level the aggregate scores.

Bill remembers: 'When David Sadler equalised, Real just couldn't believe it. They seemed to freeze, which encouraged us to attack. We got a throw on halfway and, although I was never in the habit of piling forward, something got me moving now. I said to Nobby Stiles, "Stay here, I'm going up," and he asked me what the hell I was doing. I showed for the ball but Paddy Crerand, probably unable to believe his eyes, threw it to George Best.

'Now George went down the touchline, past several tackles, and I kept going, too. As George looked up I was the only United player in the box. I thought he would never pass to me and that he would try to score at the near post. But as he feinted one way, wrong-footing the defenders, I knew what was in his mind. I had seen him do it so often.

'So I took three steps back and, sure enough, he rolled it into my path. All I had to do was side-foot it into the net. It all seemed unreal, like I was frozen in time. When everyone came to congratulate me, the first thing I did was to tell Nobby to stay back because there were still fifteen minutes to go. He said, "You miserable bugger," and George wondered why I wasn't showing any emotion. But I saved all that for later. I was just thanking God that I was in the right place and did the right thing.'

The shocked Spaniards were in no state to retaliate and United went on to face Benfica in the Wembley final, Bill winning a battle royal with the giant Portuguese centre forward Jose Torres, as a 4–1 victory was claimed in extra time.

'It was fantastic to win the European Cup, especially after what the club had been through. It was an unforgettable experience,' he said.

It might have been the perfect juncture for Bill to bow out, but still the Red Devils needed him as several young, would-be replacements failed to make the grade. Typically, he made light of his worsening injury situation to soldier on, reaching another European Cup semi-final in 1968–69, before eventually limping out of the limelight early the following term.

After that Bill turned to coaching, remaining at Old Trafford until 1974. Then, after a fleeting stint in charge of non-League Witney Town, he moved to the United States, flourishing with Chicago Sting, Tulsa Roughnecks and San Jose Earthquakes.

During the 1980s Bill became one of Norway's most accomplished coaches, tasting success with Farstad, Steinkjer, Lillestrom and Viking Stavanger, then opting for eastern horizons and reviving the fortunes of the Mazda club in Hiroshima. After three years of thriving in Japan, Bill and his wife, Teresa, returned to their native shores to live in Sale, wishing to be closer to their three children and seven grandchildren.

He is still a golfer and retains close Japanese links, frequently bringing youth sides to England from the Land of the Rising Sun, as well as being part of the Association of Former Manchester United Players, which he helped to found and then chaired for the first two years of its existence.

Chapter Twenty

BRAVE BUT BEATEN

A lthough desperately lacking experience, United's unknowns, summoned from the backwaters of the junior teams, rose to the occasion with dramatic impact.

None more so than Shay Brennan, who will forever be remembered for the two goals he scored in United's first game after the crash against Sheffield Wednesday in the FA Cup.

Mind you, there was nothing the delightful Shay, a man invariably with a smile on his face, liked better than to claim credit for another important goal in United's history. The goal that won the European Cup for Manchester United in 1968.

He would acknowledge that George Best was the scorer two minutes into extra time that sent United on their way to victory, and if pushed would concede that it wasn't a bad goal, but Shay preferred to dwell on the build-up.

With tongue firmly in his cheek he would say: 'I got this ball and knocked it back to our goalkeeper. Alex Stepney kicked it down the field, Brian Kidd headed it on and Bestie raced away to score.

'But I started the move and if I hadn't laid back that pass to Alex Stepney we wouldn't have scored ... would we?' he used to ask with a big grin, and you just had to agree.

That was Shay Brennan, a man with a bubbling, infectious sense of humour, roguishly handsome as a young man and still looking well to his dying day, on a golf course in Wexford in June of 2000.

In fact, Wilf McGuinness, his contemporary as a player and a long-time friend, regularly used to complain: 'Look at Shay, he's had a triple heart by-pass operation and he still looks better than me.'

Shay would smile and say, 'Of course, how else could it be?' and everyone loved him for it because he was arguably the most popular player United have ever had. Everybody liked him. His particular pals were Bobby Charlton, Nobby Stiles and Wilf McGuinness but all the rest loved him, too.

The fans were perhaps unaware of his popularity because he was essentially a modest, retiring man who did his best to avoid publicity and the headlines. Mind you, even Shay could do little to keep himself out of the headlines when he played on the wing to score those two goals in that fifth round 3–0 victory. He became an overnight hero and, naturally, stayed in the team for his League debut against Nottingham Forest three days later. He went on to make over 360 first-team appearances for United and won nineteen caps for the Republic of Ireland.

Although he lost his place for the FA Cup final at the end of the 1958 season, as more senior players recovered from their injuries, he shared in the success of the sixties by winning two League Championship medals and of course helping George Best score that 'winner' against Benfica in 1968.

For me, though, it was his role in helping to bridge the gap between the air crash and more normal times, thus ensuring the club's survival, that was his priceless contribution. He was always happy to play a supporting role from his normal right back position. Nothing too fancy, nothing too risky and an acceptance that there were more skilful players in the team better fitted to create the magic. Every team needs a player or two like that to knit the superstars together and make them twinkle.

Thanks to a disarming sunny nature, Shay Brennan was able to do that both on and off the field. He was known affectionately by his team-mates as 'Bomber'. When I asked Nobby Stiles why, he said he thought it must have been for the way Shay was always bombing in the goals, or rather didn't, because between his traumatic debut and his final appearance, thirteen years later, he only scored six times, and three of those were in his first season in the FA Cup. Shay was frequently at the heart of dressing room banter.

He completed his Old Trafford career in 1970 by playing in an FA Cup tie, to bring the wheel full circle. He then became player-manager of Waterford between 1970 and 1974, before settling down in nearby Tremore, where with the considerable help of his second wife, Liz, he ran a parcel courier business.

He suffered a heart attack in 1986 and successfully came through a heart by-pass operation, but fourteen years later he died suddenly at the age of sixty-three.

The scorer of the other goal against Sheffield Wednesday was another youngster hauled up from the junior teams, Alex Dawson, a tough, battling centre forward. He had made his debut, aged sixteen years and four months, before Munich and stepped up afterwards to perform valiantly. He scored in every round on the way to Wembley and that season he banged in five goals in twelve League appearances. In all he scored fifty-four goals in ninety-three League appearances for United, but he was squeezed out by the arrival of David Herd from Arsenal, though he still averaged a goal every two games, in a career that took him to Preston, Bury, Brighton and Brentford.

United have remained his club, and he is a regular visitor at the Former Players' functions at Old Trafford, from his home in Corby where he played for a final couple of seasons in non-League football.

He still has his trademark crooked nose, broken in the first League game after Munich against Nottingham Forest.

'Every time I was going to get it fixed I seemed to be transferred. I don't think an operation would have been that expensive, but every club that said let's get the nose straightened this summer followed up by selling me before I could get it done. In the end I thought, forget it. I've had a flattened nose for so long that people wouldn't recognise me if I had it straightened!'

When Albert Quixall was later signed by United for a record £45,000, he was impressed with the friendly welcome he received in the dressing room and from Alex Dawson in particular.

'I didn't know anybody but this big tough-looking guy kept winking at me and I remember thinking they were all trying to make me feel at home.' Little did Albert know that, in his younger days, Alex had something of a nervous twitch in one eye, but he might like to know it was not entirely wasted.

Mark Pearson, a small but belligerent inside forward and another of the youngsters who played a part in the survival of the club, was a raw teenager recruited from Sheffield schoolboy football who wore bushy sideburns that gave him

Back in Europe for the first time since 1958, Denis Law scores United's third goal in their 6–1 victory over Willem II in the Cup-Winners' Cup in October 1963. (*Empics*)

Seventeen-year-old George Best takes on Fulham's Bobby Keetch in March 1964. (*Getty Images*)

The ever predatory Denis Law just misses out on another goal in the game against Fulham in September 1964. However, his 28 League goals in the campaign would power United to the title by the end of the season. (*Getty Images*)

Pat Crerand rarely missed a match, and was one of the most creative forces in United's midfield during their golden period in the 1960s. (*Getty Images*)

El Beatle George Best returns from Benfica where he gave one of the greatest performances of his career to secure United's place in the European Cup semi-final in 1966. (*Empics*)

Bobby Charlton, one of the all-time greats of world football, picks up the award of European Footballer of the Year in 1966 from Matt Busby. (*Popperfoto*)

Bobby Charlton shoots for goal, despite the despairing lunge from Martin Peters. United's 6–1 win at Upton Park on 6 May 1967 was a brilliant flourish to win another League title. (*Empics*)

Nobby Stiles, tenacious as ever, tackles Jimmy Greaves during the Charity Shield game against Spurs in August 1967. (*Popperfoto*)

George Best creates havoc in the penalty area against Everton. By the end of the 1967–68 season he would be a European Cup winner, as well as the English and European Footballer of the Year. (*Getty Images*)

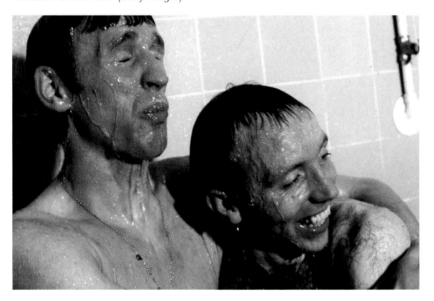

Pat Crerand and Nobby Stiles celebrate getting through to the European Cup final after drawing 3–3 against Real Madrid in Spain. (*Popperfoto*)

Goals galore! (Top) Bobby Charlton scores United's first against Benfica with a glancing header early in the second half. (Above) Brian Kidd celebrates his nineteenth birthday by scoring United's third in extra time. (*Empics/Popperfoto*)

Alex Stepney saves during the European Cup final. His late save from Eusebio was crucial in taking the game to extra time. (*Popperfoto*)

With so many famous stars on the pitch, it was actually John Aston who put in a man-of-the-match performance to help United to their 4–1 victory against Benfica. (*Empics*)

(Right) David Sadler and George Best celebrate a famous triumph; (below) while for Matt Busby and Bill Foulkes, survivors of Munich, it was the justification for all their work since that terrible tragedy. (*Empics*)

something of a bandit look and saw him nicknamed 'Pancho'. In truth there was always a bandit element to Mark's football that would see him sent off at Burnley, prompting chairman Bob Lord to describe the Old Trafford team as 'a bunch of Teddy Boys'. It was a good story at the time and it took some time for Matt Busby to get over that one. In more recent years I had to chuckle when Mark told me one of his daughters was at Nottingham University reading psychology. Said Mark: 'Yes, I can see the funny side, too. The only thing is that it was thirty years too late for me. From my point of view as a player, it was all part of growing up. There was a terrific spirit among the United players at that time after Munich. They were happy days, too, and though I later played for Sheffield Wednesday, Fulham and Halifax, the only club for me was Manchester United.'

Ian Greaves was a slightly more experienced player who answered the call. At one point pre-Munich he had kept Bill Foulkes out of the team long enough to earn a 1957 Championship medal and he proved a resolute, determined fullback, among some much younger team-mates. A knee injury slowed him down and saw him on his way into coaching at Huddersfield and an incident that established him as a man of integrity.

He explained: 'Three of my players came to see me to ask for a £30,000 bonus to keep Huddersfield in the First Division. It was quarter of an hour before kick-off and apart from being illegal in football, there was no way I was going to agree to pay money to achieve what they should already have been prepared to sweat blood for. I have always said that the epitaph I would like on my grave is one that says: "Here lies an honest man". In football it is quite easy to get sucked into cutting corners, but I have never liked fiddling.'

Ian won a lot of respect with that stance at Huddersfield. After twenty-five years as a manager and coach, he returned to Old Trafford to do some part-time scouting for Sir Alex Ferguson.

Ronnie Cope was another stalwart to come to the fore in the crisis days and he played on for a couple of seasons before moving to Luton and then joining Northwich and Winsford in the area where he still lives. Ronnie was one of those people who just loved playing football and long after his professional days were over, he could be found playing for fun with his local team.

Colin Webster, Welsh international, scored the winner against West Bromwich Albion in the fifth round replay and played in the final. He missed the Munich trip through a dose of flu and when he was transferred to Swansea midway through the next season, he triggered my first newspaper row with Matt Busby. I quoted Colin as saying that United were forcing him out, but Matt didn't like being portrayed as a bully and told me so – in his quiet but firm way.

And so this seemingly motley collection bonded together to keep Manchester United in business, reaching the Cup final and finishing a highly respectable ninth in the First Division.

They also acquitted themselves well on the European front, giving a spirited display in the first leg of their semi-final against AC Milan for a 2–1 win. The Italians scored first when Bredesen intercepted a pass to glide the ball round Harry Gregg after twenty-four minutes. It was a lead Milan deserved, but five minutes before the interval Dennis Viollet put United back in the fight by snapping up a half-chance in the box from a mishit back-pass. With Murphy no doubt winding up his players during the interval, United came out to launch themselves at the Italians with a blazing fury.

Schiaffino was now sporting a big plaster over a cut eye, the result of a collision with Gregg, and his team began to waver. Goodwin and Taylor forced Buffoni to make great saves and Webster shot high as the Reds tore into the opposition. United grabbed their winner just eleven minutes from the end, after Viollet had been brought down by Maldini. The centre half flung himself to the ground in anguish and his team-mates protested violently as Danish referee Helge awarded a penalty.

But all that meant nothing to little Ernie Taylor, who stayed cool amid the scenes of excitement, to smash his spot-kick into the goal off the underside of the crossbar. It was victory on the night but a slender lead and it proved far from enough as United crashed to a 4–0 defeat in the second leg. Little went right for them. To start with, for obvious reasons, they had travelled overland by boat and train to Milan, not ideal preparation for an examination in the mighty San Siro Stadium.

At first they couldn't even gain entry to the ground as their coach was turned away from a succession of gates until they found the 'right' entrance. They didn't reach their dressing room until twenty-five minutes before the kick-off in a ground filled with a volatile crowd. The players felt it was gamesmanship to upset them and they also had to deal with some surprising decisions from the German referee Albert Deutsch but Harry Gregg admitted: 'Milan were really a class above us.'

United withstood the pressure in the first half, but the fact that it took them until nearly half time to win their first corner tells the story. Four minutes into the second half Schiaffino lobbed Gregg. Ronnie Cope saved on the line but conceded a penalty, for handling, which Liedholm converted.

Schiaffino went on to score twice, with the other goal coming from Danova.

Young Kenny Morgans had recovered from his injuries in time to play in the semi-final, but that didn't compensate for the absence of Bobby Charlton, who was somewhat harshly taken by England for an end of season tour involving friendly matches.

Even the experienced Bill Foulkes found the game in Milan an intimidating experience.

'The Italian crowd didn't show us much sympathy. As we walked out we were bombarded with vegetables. I remember being hit by cabbages and the biggest bunch of carrots I have ever seen. It was very hostile with all the flares and fireworks. Milan had a good team, too, with players like Schiaffino and Liedholm, and they crushed us in the second half.

'It was a sad end to a horrific season, but inevitable when you think about it. Emotion and spirit had kept us going for a long time, but after a while it was not enough. I know that in the summer I was happy just to rest and count my good fortune, that I was at least playing football, while so many of my friends and team-mates just hadn't made it.'

Chapter Twenty-one

LIKE A PHOENIX

Harold Hardman had made it quite clear from the start, even when everyone was reeling from the shock of Munich, that Manchester United would recover like the symbolic phoenix they wore on their jerseys for the FA Cup final at the end of their tragic season.

He had declared: 'Although we mourn our dead and grieve for our wounded we believe that great days are not done for us. The sympathy and encouragement of the football world and particularly of our supporters will justify and inspire us. The road back may be long and hard but with the memory of those who died at Munich, of their stirring achievements and wonderful sportsmanship ever with us, Manchester United will rise again.'

The first faltering steps had been taken under the inspired leadership of the seventy-year-old Hardman and Jimmy Murphy while Matt Busby had fought for his life. But the maestro was back for the 1958–59 season, encouraged by Jean who told him that, though he couldn't bear the thought of having anything more to do with football, he must go back.

'Those boys who died expect it of you,' she told him and it wasn't long before he was in the thick of it, bringing Albert Quixall to Old Trafford from Sheffield Wednesday.

Albert was something of a golden boy in his day, fabulously skilful and playing for the full England team by the age of eighteen. He deserves to be talked about in the same breath as more obvious legends because he kept alive United's traditional style of playing creative, attacking football with flair, at a time when it was inevitably spread pretty thinly.

At least there was plenty of aggression coming from the half back line behind him, with Wilf McGuinness now winning a regular place in the team. Wilf had captained the England schoolboy team with Bobby Charlton under his command and he was clearly going to be an important player for United, until a badly broken leg at the age of twenty-two ended his career for both club and country after winning two caps.

A splendid and enthusiastic character he was a natural coach and joined the United staff as well as helping Sir Alf Ramsey prepare the players for the 1966 World Cup. He was highly thought of and picked to follow Busby as manager, but it didn't work out at United and he left for management jobs with Aris Salonika in Greece, York and Hull before taking up physiotherapy at Bury. Nowadays he is a successful after-dinner speaker and MC as well as coming home to Old Trafford as the pundit on Manchester United Radio.

Also back on the scene that season was Albert Scanlon, recovered from his Munich injuries, and he was back with a bang to score sixteen goals as a League ever-present at outside left in what was a sensational season. To finish runners-up so soon after the crash was incredible. It was certainly a marvellous return for the locally born Scanlon, but he only had one

more season before seeming to lose his way, which prompted a transfer to Newcastle before spells with Lincoln and Mansfield.

After football he cut something of a lonely figure and some years ago he explained to me: 'I like to wander round the ground remembering things. I don't bother anyone. I don't know any of the management anyway, no reason why they should know me either. But I still feel part of Manchester United. I expect I shall die that way. I have only been in the players' lounge once since I left and that was when they had a reunion of the Munich players. But I like to go back. The club have been good to me over the years with tickets for matches but I do like to wander around. I used to look at the pylon Jeff Whitefoot once climbed. That's gone now. I see the part of the stand where Tommy Taylor once trained on his own and every-one forgot about him. He was missing for four hours. The memories come back for me. I just hope that no one ever puts a hand on my shoulder and stops me. I don't expect people recognise me after all the years and the changes, but it would really hurt me if someone said I had no business being there.'

I have always felt that the crash shortened Albert's career. As he says: 'I played afterwards but I couldn't change as the game changed. New players had to be brought in after Munich and I never adapted. After I finished football I worked for fif-teen years at Salford Docks until they shut down, then as a security guard in Trafford Park just round the corner from the ground.'

But he certainly did well enough in that first full season after the crash, as did another remarkable player on the other wing, Warren Bradley, United's footballing headmaster. He was Flying Officer Bradley stationed at Flying Training

Command, Hucknall, Nottingham, when he first heard the news from Munich, news that would change his life. Because he had been to Durham University, Warren had played his football with Bishop Auckland and their inside forward, Derek Lewin, who had trained under Jimmy Murphy with the British Olympic team in 1956, thought a few of them might be able to help out. The result was that Derek, Warren and Bobby Hardisty, all England amateur internationals, agreed to play for United's reserves until they had sorted themselves out.

But Busby liked what he saw in Bradley who by now, with National Service completed, was looking to start his teaching career. He asked him to try for a job in the Manchester area so he started at Greatstone Secondary School in Stretford, and shortly afterwards signed on as a part-time professional for the Reds.

Warren, successfully combining the two jobs, scored twelve goals in twenty-four games in his first season playing in a highly productive forward line with Albert Quixall, Dennis Viollet, Bobby Charlton and Albert Scanlon. It was undoubtedly this high-scoring attack (totalling more than a hundred) that saw them finish second to Wolves. I remember writing at the time that Walter Winterbottom could do worse than pick that United forward line for England. Well, he didn't go quite that far but fifteen months after Munich he gave Warren the first of his three caps and he lined up with Bobby Charlton and Johnny Haynes against Italy to become the only player to appear for England at full and amateur levels in the same season.

How did the officer and teacher get on with his team-mates?

Wilf McGuinness says: 'A few of us wondered how this amateur university lad would fare in the real professional world, but he quickly put us in our place with the kind of performances that not only got him into our first team, but into the England side as well. United didn't get many university boys in those days but he was popular in the dressing room because he didn't have any fancy airs or graces. We also quickly came to respect him as a player which, in the professional game, is what really matters.'

Wilf was playing in a reserve match with Warren when he suffered the fractured leg that ended his career. Says Warren: 'I can still recall hearing the crack of the bone breaking.'

The emergence of Johnny Giles squeezed Bradley out of the United team after sixty-three League games and twenty goals. He joined Bury, but knee injuries and the growing demands of teaching brought an end to his football career. He went on to hold three inner-city headships in Manchester and Bolton before retiring to set up his own educational management consultancy. He now lives near Bolton and is treasurer of the Former Players Association. With a teaching career as rewarding as his days as a footballer, he went back to Durham University a few years ago to be made an Honorary Palatinate along with another sporting luminary, Frank 'Typhoon' Tyson, the fast bowler who in 1955 had blitzed the Australian batting to retain the Ashes.

United's form dipped after finishing runners-up in 1959 and after a particularly heavy thrashing when they lost 7–3 at Newcastle in January 1960, Busby went into the transfer market to buy Maurice Setters, the bandy-legged, tough-tackling midfielder, for £30,000 from West Bromwich Albion.

A no-nonsense player, he didn't have much time for what he considered to be the fancy-Dan style of Quixall and he wasn't shy in ripping into my match reports either. A few times, as I boarded the team coach bound for an away game, I would be greeted by a voice from the back of the bus telling me that what I had written in the 'Pink' the previous week was crap. Just once I delivered the perfect response. Maurice was out of the team at the time, feeling the challenge of the emerging Nobby Stiles, and I replied: 'If you thought a bit more about football instead of slagging me off, you might even get back into the team!' I earned a ripple of applause for that one from his team-mates. Not that it stopped Maurice for very long. He enjoyed a long and well-travelled career, excelling as assistant to Jack Charlton when he was manager of the Republic of Ireland.

United certainly needed his presence, because they were beginning to feel the pinch. My editor, Tom Henry, was so upset by the Newcastle defeat that without telling anyone he changed the 'United thrashed' headline that had been written for that night's 'Pink'. He was a bit of a United fan and used his position of editor to slip in the new headline: 'United in 10-goal thriller'. True, I suppose, and certainly kinder than the original!

United finished seventh that season and likewise the following year, though not without bringing in yet another ready-made recruit. This time it was the experienced Noel Cantwell, a tall fullback, a Republic of Ireland international, a real student of the game and a natural captain and leader.

Capped thirty-six times for the Republic, the Cork-born Irishman belonged to that hothouse of strategists who were trying to set the soccer world alight at West Ham during the late fifties. Men like Malcolm Allison, John Bond, Malcolm Musgrove, Dave Sexton, Frank O'Farrell and Bobby Moore used to gather after training at a little café called Casetari's

round the corner from their ground. There they would move the salt and pepper pots around the table as they discussed tactics. It was a finishing school for future managers. Indeed, three of them went on to become either a manager or coach at Old Trafford and Noel Cantwell was one of the leading disciples among Upton Park's footballing free-thinkers.

So when Matt Busby paid West Ham the record fee for a fullback of £29,500, his new environment came as something of a culture shock. Intelligent, articulate and full of ideas about the game, he couldn't wait for the opportunity to learn from the most respected manager in football and get down to talking about the way forward with his illustrious new team-mates. He had a long wait because, sadly for Noel, Manchester United was not that kind of club. Busby didn't believe in smothering his players with tactics. He relied instead on their intuition and concentrated on gathering round him players with the natural talent to express themselves, rather than trying to recall instructions from a dossier.

Noel, perhaps slightly disillusioned, nevertheless fitted in perfectly at left back to become the obvious man to captain the side through a testing time. For this was the crucial period after the Munich crash when having steadied the ship by signing players like Ernie Taylor, Albert Quixall and Maurice Setters, Busby needed to build further if he was to get back among the honours. Cantwell arrived in November 1960 and more than played his part in leading United to their first trophy after the disaster. He was the defensive cornerstone and with the help of later arrivals like David Herd, Denis Law and Pat Crerand, United rose superbly to the occasion as underdogs in the 1963 FA Cup final against Leicester City.

It was the launch pad for the great era of the sixties,

and though Noel Cantwell had faded before the later Championship successes, he had been instrumental in bridging the barren years after the air crash. He was a natural choice as chairman of the Professional Footballers Association and many thought he would succeed Matt Busby as manager at Old Trafford, but instead he left to become manager of Coventry City as well as enjoying a spell as manager of the Republic of Ireland. He later managed in the United States and at Peterborough where he settled and ran a pub.

He eventually retired from the pub business and, much to his delight, came back into football to help the England international team as a scout for the Football Association. His immediate boss was another United old boy, Dave Sexton, manager at Old Trafford from 1977 to 1981. Noel told me: 'I'm one of a team directed by Dave Sexton who travel around assessing opposition and making form reports on England players.'

Sadly Noel died just before Christmas 2005, after a brave fight against a cancer that had started at the site of an old leg injury.

Chapter Twenty-two

BACK AMONG THE HONOURS

———

S lowly but surely Busby began to fit the pieces together. Nobby Stiles broke through to become a regular, but the manager still felt he had to turn to the transfer market and his next big signing was David Herd for £35,000 from Arsenal for the start of season 1961–62. David was never really given the status of legend because he played under the shadow cast by those super luminaries, Best, Law and Charlton, but really he deserves to be ranked up there with the greatest.

For what David Herd gave the team was priceless, a virtually guaranteed twenty League goals a season, which is what he did at Old Trafford for almost six years. In his first season he contributed 14 goals from 27 appearances. Then, with the arrival of Denis Law as a regular partner, he reeled off seasonal totals of 19, 20, 20 and 24. In his sixth season he was on 16 but broke his leg. As it was only March, without the injury it could well have been his best-ever scoring season.

As Pat Crerand will still tell you: 'David Herd was one of the most underrated players ever to play for Manchester United.'

That's how he figured with me, too, a strong runner who

knew his way to goal and had a powerful shot. Typically it was in the act of scoring a goal when he broke his leg in March 1967. He had dispatched the ball goalwards from just outside the penalty area when his leg caught Graham Cross, as the Leicester player slid across him in an attempt to block the shot. The leg was completely broken with his foot hanging limply at an angle and it was the beginning of the end of his career. He managed two more seasons at Stoke, following the route taken by a number of United players like Harry Gregg and Dennis Viollet, leaving Matt Busby for the irrepressible Tony Waddington.

Busby had played with Alex Herd at Manchester City and followed fifteen-year-old David's career closely at Stockport County, where he played alongside his dad. David had five seasons at Edgeley Park before moving to Highbury for £8,000 where he continued to score goals. In his final season at Arsenal he scored thirty League goals, second only to Jimmy Greaves as the First Division's highest scorer and he certainly gave United an important scoring boost.

The team was taking on a new look, with David Herd scoring up front, Noel Cantwell steadying the defence, Maurice Setters a power in midfield and youngsters Nobby Stiles and Johnny Giles looking good. However, Busby knew he still needed a stronger side if he was ever to get back to the standard set by his beloved Babes.

At the beginning of season 1962–63 he pulled off his most audacious signing of all, by paying yet another record fee to bring Denis Law back home from exile in Italy. Matt knew all about Denis. Indeed he had tried to buy him from Bill Shankly after watching him play for Huddersfield against United in a youth match and then watched in frustration when he was sold to Manchester City and from there to Torino. But a great deal of persistence – and £115,000 – finally got Busby his man.

The new partnership up front of Herd and Law scored a goal apiece in a 2–2 home draw against West Bromwich Albion on the opening day of the season, but the team still lacked consistency. In fact, they were losing more matches than they were winning and Matt decided that it was all very well having two big guns up front but that the right kind of ammunition wasn't reaching them often enough. So he ventured into the transfer market once more to bring Pat Crerand to Old Trafford from Glasgow Celtic for £55,000.

As so often happens in football, the team looked good on paper but they lost four on the bounce to mark Crerand's arrival as they slowly slid towards the relegation area. There was even talk of the sack for Matt Busby and when I went to see chairman Harold Hardman for a vote of confidence and to hear him dismiss the speculation as rubbish, word of my visit got back to the manager and he was angry at what he perceived as the local reporter going behind his back. That's how much the pressure was getting to Matt as he strived to rebuild the shattered club.

Happily for all concerned redemption lay just around the corner in the shape of the FA Cup. Denis Law scored a hat trick in a 5–0 win against Huddersfield at Old Trafford in the opening third round and suddenly everything began to fall into place. Albert Quixall enjoyed a revival and scored in each of the first four rounds as the Reds knocked out Aston Villa, Chelsea and Coventry before Law dispatched Southampton 1–0 in the semi-final at Villa Park.

So United fans now had the excitement of a day out at Wembley and could put their League worries behind them. And they were happy to do so, because the team was certainly still stuttering in the First Division with four defeats, two wins and a draw in the run-up to the final. Although they had done well in the Cup, their League form saw them go to Wembley as underdogs. Leicester, on the other hand – at one point challenging for the Championship – were expected to swamp a team heading for a finishing place of nineteenth in the League table.

Wembley proved a revelation, a lifeline, as United stormed to a 3–1 victory to collect their first trophy since the crash. It had been a long, hard five years but suddenly there was hope as everything clicked into place to suggest that this might just be the start of something really big.

United's potential flowered on that warm sunny day with new boys Law and Crerand revelling in the wide open spaces of Wembley. It was from one of Crerand's slide-rule passes that Law swivelled to beat Gordon Banks with a low shot to put the Reds ahead after twenty-nine minutes. David Herd, never out of any scoring picture for long, scored after fifty-eight minutes and although Ken Keyworth pulled a goal back for Leicester, Herd pounced again to make it a convincing 3–1 victory.

It seemed as if the jigsaw was complete with Crerand the final piece to make the team tick. The attack now looked capable of providing a more consistent scoring level. With Crerand operating in midfield, there was a good balance in the half back line, with Maurice Setters the ball-winner on one flank and the Scot, a player of vision, on the other. The transfer was one of Busby's shrewdest decisions.

Crerand had arrived too late in his first season to do much about the League position. Indeed, he struggled to fit in at first, but in the FA Cup that season there developed a pattern and a glimpse of better days ahead. The final was the match that saw Crerand come into his own and he destroyed the Leicester midfield in a link-up with Law that was a firm indication of things to come.

Manchester United and Pat Crerand were on their way, as they showed the following season, by finishing runners-up in the First Division and reaching the FA Cup semi-finals again, as well as enjoying a decent run in the European Cup Winners Cup.

The next three seasons brought them two Championships and the European Cup, with Crerand at the heart of their super side of the sixties. It was sometimes said he was slow and a favourite jibe from after-dinner speakers these days is that he had two speeds, slow and stop! But the remark doesn't do justice to his superbly creative skills.

The Scot also had his fiery moments. He once escaped a ban after hitting an opponent on the grounds that he had only struck him once, which hardly constituted fighting. What was not mentioned was that where Pat Crerand was concerned, nothing more then one punch was ever needed – as the goalkeeper who never made it to the top of the tunnel after a European match could testify!

After a brief spell as assistant manager to Tommy Docherty at Old Trafford and a few other coaching posts at the end of his playing career, Pat remains an ardent United fan.

Pat Crerand, once the heartbeat of Manchester United out on the pitch, is now their passionate advocate on television. He has become as integral to the commentary team on Manchester United TV as he was to the glory side of the sixties, when it was said that if Crerand played well, United played well. In all he made 304 League appearances for United and scored ten goals. He won sixteen caps for Scotland, still avidly follows Celtic's results, but is now a firmly adopted Mancunian living in Sale, just a few miles down the road from Old Trafford.

Chapter Twenty-three

THE LAWMAN

The great football trinity of Charlton, Law and Best was beginning to come together, with George, the new boy, making his debut the season after the FA Cup win, Bobby Charlton the thread running through the Busby era, and Denis Law lighting up the team with his explosive goal scoring and warrior style of play that soon made him the hero of the Stretford End.

Denis was 'The King', the people's champion with a fervour that matched the passion of the supporters who found it so easy to identify with him. They liked the venom in his play and they liked the streak of villainy which saw him serve two six-week suspensions in the course of his career. They loved his willingness to fly into the thick of the action. He was daring, cocky, impudent and abrasive, which together with his flair for being in the right place at the right time and his prolific goal scoring was an explosive mix that made him a popular hero.

Each was a star, in that great side of the sixties, in his own right. Bobby Charlton was admired, George Best was fêted, but Law was worshipped because he brought together flair and fire.

The trinity of Charlton, Law and Best still trips easily off the tongue and the trio are such a part of United's history that the club are planning to commission a statue of the three of them together, three European Footballers of the Year who played in the same team at the same time. Watching them at the time, we didn't really know how lucky we were.

Denis Law was also much admired back home in Scotland and bearing in mind that Scottish footballers plying their trade in England have not always been popular north of the border, this was some achievement, but Denis *was* different. Only a few years ago, he was voted Scotland's greatest ever football player, crowned the top Scot at a ceremony in Glasgow following a poll by readers of the influential *Daily Record* newspaper. Long known as 'The King' in Manchester, Denis now reigns monarch of the glens after a vote that saw him hold off the challenge of Kenny Dalgleish and the popular Jim Baxter in a poll to name the Hampden heroes.

He was handed his award by former team-mate Sir Bobby Charlton at a Hampden Park ceremony attended by Chancellor Gordon Brown and Sir Alex Ferguson, who delighted the Tartan Army when he said the greatest ever Scotland team would beat any all-time England side and referred to the strike partnership of Law and Dalglish as made in Heaven.

'Dalglish or Law would score in the first minute, then they would give the ball to Jimmy "Jinky" Johnstone and the other lot wouldn't get it off him until the final whistle,' declared the Manchester United chief who was himself voted the greatest ever Scottish manager.

Law said: 'At this stage of my life it's fantastic to receive such an honour. When I think of all the great players who have graced the Scottish jersey, and I have played with many of them, like Jim Baxter and Kenny Dalgleish, then I'm thrilled the *Record* readers have chosen me.'

Denis flourished in front of goal, where his scoring rate over a long period makes him the most deadly marksman of all the famous players to perform on the Old Trafford stage. His strike rate was phenomenal in all competitions. Playing for United he scored 171 goals from 305 League games, 34 FA Cup goals in 44 appearances and 28 goals in 33 European matches.

Sir Bobby Charlton scored a record 198 times but it took him 604 games to do it, while, for all his magic, George Best had a ratio of 137 goals from 361 appearances. David Herd hit 144 goals in 263 appearances; impressive, but nobody can quite touch the Lawman.

Even compared with the present day his record stands scrutiny. Ruud van Nistelrooy is clearly well on his way towards challenging Law's return after already matching his European total and, significantly, doing it in four fewer games. Van Nistelrooy's League strike rate is also impressive as he moves steadily towards a League century of goals, but he has some way to go yet before he reaches Law's career total. Playing for Scotland Denis scored thirty goals in fifty-five appearances and few fans from the sixties will forget the Law trademark as he signalled his goals to the crowd, punching the air and wheeling away with arm raised, his hand clutching his sleeve, save for the one finger pointing to the sky to acknowledge the goal. The terrace fans would rise to his salute as to a gladiator of old.

Yet few would have predicted a glittering career looking at the fragile youngster who had a bad squint. Nonetheless, he showed enough ability to attract the attention of Archie Beattie in Scotland, whose brother, Andy, was manager of

Huddersfield Town. Bill Shankly, who was then in charge of Huddersfield's reserves before becoming manager, said later: 'He looked like a skinned rabbit. My first reaction was to say get him on the next train home.'

But after his trial, Huddersfield saw enough to take him on to their ground staff as an apprentice in April 1955 and life got even better after an operation cured the 'lazy eye' that had forced him to play a lot of the time with one eye closed. As he explains in his autobiography: 'I cannot emphasise enough what an incredible moment in my life that was. It completely changed things for me. Suddenly I had the wherewithal to look people, literally, straight in the eye, something I had never been able to do with any confidence before.

'I returned to Huddersfield after a couple of weeks' convalescence, and it was a great feeling just to go into the ground with the rest of the lads and be normal. Wow! And I could now play football with both eyes open.'

Denis was soon in Huddersfield's youth team, which was when he caught the eye of Matt Busby in an FA Youth Cup tie against Manchester United. Huddersfield lost, but Busby after the game offered Andy Beattie £10,000 for his sixteen-year-old forward, a remarkably generous offer for such a young player.

The bid was turned down because Huddersfield had other plans and on Christmas Eve 1956, their promising apprentice was given his League debut at inside right against Notts County aged sixteen years and ten months, the youngest player Huddersfield had ever fielded.

There was also an arrogance suggesting he could perform on a bigger stage and Matt Busby, enjoying a brief spell as manager of Scotland, capped him against Wales at Ninian Park, Cardiff, on 18 October 1958 where he marked the occasion by scoring in a 3–0 win. In December 1959, Shankly left to become manager of Liverpool and speculation mounted that the up-and-coming Law would also be leaving, with Everton, Arsenal, Chelsea and Glasgow Rangers all reported as interested. It was in fact Manchester City who landed him, paying £55,000 on 15 March 1960, a British record transfer fee.

The Scot did well at Maine Road, but did not need much persuading to leave City, when Torino scout Gigi Peronace arrived on the scene to offer him a £5,000 signing-on fee plus a £200 win bonus. Such a lira lure compared well with the English maximum wage of £20 a week, though this was set to change. City collected a record £110,000 fee for his transfer in June 1961, but the Italian move proved a disaster. Denis just couldn't settle and he was irked by what he considered to be the restrictions Italy imposed on their footballers. His time in Italy was hardly a sunshine holiday, especially after a car crash when he and Joe Baker attempted to go round a roundabout the wrong way and flipped the car over.

He let it be known that he longed to return to English football and on 12 July 1962, after a lengthy chase by Matt Busby, he arrived at Manchester United for £115,000.

His first season of 1962–63 saw United flirt with relegation, but Law did enjoy winning the FA Cup against Leicester, a trophy in his first season with a new club, not bad going, and he described his own performance at Wembley as one of his greatest games in a red shirt.

His real breakthrough came the following season, though, with new signing Pat Crerand coming into his own to give Law improved support and help him score thirty League goals from forty-one games. It was a bravura performance that made him the 1964 European Footballer of the Year.

Honours came thick and fast for Law in United's super side of the sixties. They won the Championship in 1964–65 with Law top scorer on twenty-eight and they made everyone sit up the following year by reaching the semi-finals of the European Cup, losing unaccountably to Partizan Belgrade after beating Benfica in the quarter-final.

George Best had grabbed the headlines against Benfica in the second leg in Lisbon in a 5–1 victory and Law says: 'It was the best performance in my view from a United team in Europe. It was a beautiful experience and a joy to share in that splendid team effort. Matt Busby called it "our finest hour" and I think he summed it up well.'

Denis top scored again the following year (1966–67) as United won the League to earn another crack at the European Cup, which of course they won – but without Denis, who was in Manchester for an operation as his team-mates beat Benfica at Wembley in the final.

Missing the final was a bitter blow after contributing so much towards getting United to Wembley, but at least the operation solved the mystery of the knee problem that had plagued him for so long and which some people had been suggesting was more in his mind than in his leg.

As Denis puts it in his book *The King*: 'Racehorses received better treatment than we did. Football's idea of curing an injury was to use cortisone injections. When injected into your body it disguised pain for three or four hours, converted into cortisol and influenced the nutrition and growth of connective tissues.

'The advice now is not to have more than one a month, with a maximum of three or four during the course of a year and to avoid excessive movement or stress on the joint for about a week, but we were injected and told to go straight out and play.

'I seemed to have one every week. I used to come into the dressing room at half time with my knee aching and throbbing and I would sit in the big bath with a hosepipe spraying cold water on it in an effort to deaden the pain. That was the extent of my treatment. Then I would get out of the bath and go out and play.

'The most expensive player on United's books and that was how I was treated. And not just me, I hasten to add, everybody was treated the same. Do that for a season or two seasons, just to deaden the pain, with regular cortisone injections and it will begin to take its toll. It was and should have been unacceptable, but we put up with it.

'George Best was into all that as well for a long time with his bad knee: injections, hot and cold water and aspirins. Looking back on it now, it's hard to believe. Nowadays clubs have realised how valuable their playing assets are; the training ground at Manchester United is just phenomenal, with physios, doctors, medical equipment, ultrasound – everything a finely tuned athlete needs.'

A visit to a Harley Street specialist finally came up with the possibility that the surgeon who had taken out his cartilage when he was playing for Huddersfield had failed to extract the entire piece of gristle and that this had been knocked loose and was the source of the aggravation.

The result was that after being ruled unfit for the final of the European Cup he went into hospital for what was supposed to be an exploratory operation but they pulled out a piece of floating cartilage, put it in a jar and gave it to him. It was an inch and a half long.

And they said it had all been in his mind!

As for the final, the nurses at St Joseph's Hospital were United supporters and he tells us: 'A few of my pals came in too and along with the nurses we watched the match in my room and got bladdered together on a case of McEwans. It was a great emotional night for everyone. I took the congratulations from my friends, the nursing staff and other patients, but it wasn't about me; it was about Sir Matt, a decade after he had lain on what he must have thought was his deathbed. The cheers were soon mixed with tears as Matt Busby finally held aloft the European Cup.'

After a final season back at Maine Road with Manchester City following a free transfer from Tommy Docherty, Denis became a familiar voice on radio and television as well as making celebrity appearances and appearing on the sportsmen's speaking circuit.

Sir Matt used to describe him as a good friend and a warm-hearted family man who is never less than cheerful. The year 2005 saw his spirit tested but he won through like the king he is after an operation for prostate cancer, and he is now fit and well. His popularity, like his spirit, remains undimmed. This last year saw two books published about him, an official autobiography written with Bob Harris and one penned by local Manchester author and boxing coach Brian Hughes, from the perspective of a fan.

Both are appropriately titled: *The King*.

What else!

Chapter Twenty-four

SIR BOBBY

'When things looked their blackest after the Munich accident and there were times when I felt great despair, I was enormously cheered to think that Bobby Charlton was there. His presence was a great source of inspiration to keep working for the restoration of Manchester United.'

Those are the heartfelt words of Matt Busby and they somehow sum up the career of a world-renowned footballer in an association with Manchester United that goes back over fifty years and has seen him move from apprentice to director. It's difficult to know which is the appropriate stage in this tale of United legends to introduce such an influential character, one whose story is so closely woven into the history of Old Trafford.

Perhaps now is the moment, because the two Championships in the run-up to the European Cup final and the game against Benfica were the culmination of his time, man and boy, with Manchester United.

He is arguably the most famous footballer in the world and

I always smile when I think back to being on the team coach travelling from West Berlin to the Russian sector to play the Red Army team of Vorwaerts in the European Cup and we were held up at Checkpoint Charlie.

The guards were grim-looking and it didn't improve their mood when one of our players filled his form in under the name of James Bond. It looked as if we were going to be stuck there for ages, but suddenly they realised Bobby Charlton was on board and as if by magic the frowns turned to smiles and in exchange for his autograph we sailed through, and still with Pat '007' Crerand on board!

Bobby is famous not just for his record of playing in 754 games, his thunderbolt goals and his distinguished England career, but for the grace and beauty of the way he played as a great Corinthian. He had a sporting spirit which saw him commit only one disciplinary offence in the whole of his career, and that was a booking for failing to retreat at a free kick which was subsequently wiped off his record by the Football Association as a mistake!

He was, and still is, an idol without feet of clay, a gentleman and a sportsman supreme whose behaviour was exemplary both on and off the field; and even today in his life and career following his time as a player he is just as distinguished, successful and respected.

He played in every European tie of season 1967–68 and truly made his mark in the final by scoring twice. His first came with a header, perhaps a happy omen because he didn't score too many that way. His second made the match safe at 4–1 to secure the great European victory that had been the dream of Sir Matt Busby since defying authority to lead English football into European football in 1956. Much had happened along the way and the final was played out against a highly charged emotional background, especially for those who had been in the Munich tragedy.

Beating Benfica put Manchester United into the record books as the first English team to win the European Cup following the success of Glasgow Celtic for Scotland the year before, but the drama had a huge impact on Bobby Charlton. After the match the players met up with their families and friends to celebrate at the Russell Hotel, but Bobby felt so drained he stayed in his room.

It was always likely that Bobby Charlton would become a soccer player, given that his mother, Cissie, came from the famous Milburn soccer family in the North East of England. Three of her brothers, Jack, Jim and George, played for Leeds United, while a fourth, Stan, played for Leicester City. Cissie's cousin was the legendary Newcastle United centre forward 'Wor' Jackie Milburn, while her grandfather 'Tanner' Milburn kept goal for his local team.

It was hardly surprising then that first Bobby's brother, Jack, grew up to play for Leeds United and England while Bobby himself soon attracted attention as a schoolboy and went on to enjoy an even more famous career. Born in Northumberland, the sons of a miner in the coal pit village of Ashington, Bobby and Jack went to the local junior school where their first football shorts were run up by one of the lady teachers from wartime blackout curtaining.

Manchester United heard about Bobby and on 9 February 1953 sent their chief scout, Joe Armstrong, to watch him in a game. Joe came dashing back to announce: 'I had to peer through a mist, but what I saw was enough. This boy is going to be a world beater.'

Later when he had begun to score goals for the England schoolboy team, scouts from all over came with offers for him to sign. At one stage there were said to be as many as eighteen clubs interested, but he'd made a promise to Joe Armstrong and came to Manchester United.

He first caught the eye of United fans playing in three successive FA Youth Cup-winning teams, then became a regular reserve, scoring frequently. They must have wondered when he was going to get a chance in the first team. The call finally came for a debut against Charlton Athletic at Old Trafford on 6 October 1956 and Bobby took a gamble. 'Mr Busby asked me if I was OK. Actually I had a sprained ankle but I wasn't going to admit to it and I crossed my fingers and said yes,' he explained. He did well enough, scoring twice in a 4–2 win, though he was dropped for the following match at Sunderland, one week later, to make way for the return of Tommy Taylor after injury.

Competition was severe as the Busby Babes came through and at first Bobby played only when there was an injury to Taylor, Dennis Viollet or Billy Whelan in the forward line. Gradually, though, his appearances became more regular and towards the end of the 1956–57 season, he settled into the side, making a total of fourteen appearances. His eye for goal was remarkable and though surrounded by more experienced players, he made his presence felt, netting ten times during a victorious season in the newly emerging Babes side.

Bobby also won a place in the FA Cup team for the later stages of the 1956–57 season, scoring in the semi-final win against Birmingham City and then playing in the final against Aston Villa when United seemed set to achieve a League and

Cup double until goalkeeper Ray Wood had his cheekbone smashed in the McParland incident.

Charlton, still only eighteen, also made his debut in the European Cup that season, with a prominent display for such a young player in the 2–2 semi-final second leg against Real Madrid on 25 April. It was a vintage era and it needed a special talent to break into a side which seemed to score goals at will and indeed had rattled in 103 on their way to winning the League.

It meant he still had to fight for a permanent place and it didn't come until midway through the following season. When he got in, though, he really made his mark, such as a hat trick in a 7–2 home win over Bolton on 18 January and scoring both goals in an FA Cup fourth round tie, won 2–0 at Old Trafford against Ipswich the following week.

He also took Europe in an effortless stride that season when he played in the first leg of the European Cup quarter-final against Red Star Belgrade at Old Trafford. He scored in a 2–1 win to book a trip for the fateful second leg in Belgrade. He scored twice in the 3–3 draw which secured United a place in the semi-finals and, like the rest of the young men flying home the following day for Saturday's match against Wolves, the football world lay at his feet.

But then came the heart-breaking tragedy of the crash. Bobby was knocked out and was dragged clear of the wreckage by team-mate Harry Gregg. He was kept in hospital suffering from concussion, shock and cuts, but he was relatively fortunate. He was sent home to rest on arriving back in England but returned to action for the FA Cup sixth round against West Bromwich on 1 March to help the poignantly patched-up team go all the way to the final.

Then began the long and difficult process of rebuilding. Players came and went but Charlton was a constant. Indeed, many felt that he had gone out to Belgrade a boy, but after the experience of Munich quickly became a man.

He certainly threw himself into playing for his club and in the season after Munich, 1958–59, played thirty-eight League games and scored twenty-eight goals. He played mostly on the left wing at this time, a position he didn't particularly like because he didn't feel involved enough. He was still on the wing in the team which beat Leicester to win the FA Cup in 1963, but by season 1964–65 Matt Busby had moved him into a midfield position wearing the number eight shirt. He became more influential and his skills as a creative player as well as a marksman were given more rein. He was a key figure in the Championship success of that season. His scoring rate dropped, but his passing pulled defences apart and his ability to ghost past opponents with grace, acceleration and ease was lovely to watch.

It was at this stage that his international career reached a peak. He had made his England debut just a few months after the Munich accident, playing against Scotland at Hampden, and over the next twelve years he won 106 caps while scoring forty-nine goals, a scoring record which still stands. His great year came in 1966 when two typical Charlton goals against Portugal, fierce shots which gave the goalkeeper no chance, put England through to the final of the World Cup.

Charlton was a tireless and inspired player at Wembley in the final against West Germany. His relentless foraging, telling passes and scoring threat caused problems throughout the match and made sure that the German half back, Franz Beckenbauer, had little time to prompt his own forwards.

Normal time finished level at 1–1 and then in extra time the fluency of Charlton went a long way towards helping Geoff Hurst score his famous World Cup final hat trick, for a 4–2 victory. Bobby, who confirmed his world-class ranking, shared the pitch with his brother Jack. The climax was tearful but Bobby wouldn't be ashamed of that.

Soon after the 1966 international triumph he was voted Footballer of the Year by England's soccer writers, an honour quickly followed by European Footballer of the Year, as well as an award from the referees as a Model Player.

Bobby Charlton was not finished with honours yet, though. He was in his pomp now and was one of the outstanding players along with Denis Law, David Herd, George Best, Nobby Stiles and Alex Stepney who won the Championship of 1966–67. He was a League ever-present and scored twelve goals from midfield to qualify for another crack in Europe. This was the pinnacle of his career as United swept to their great European Cup triumph of 1968. Bobby felt it was the club's destiny to become champions of Europe that season, exactly ten years after Munich.

'My thoughts on the day of the final against Benfica were that we had come too far and been through too much for us to fail in that final game,' he declared.

In all he played First Division football for seventeen seasons: making a club record of 604 appearances and scoring a record 199 goals. In 1973 he retired and he was elected a director of United in 1984. He was knighted in the birthday honours of 1994 after being awarded an OBE and CBE in the course of a distinguished career which didn't just end with football.

He had a brief foray into management at Preston but

moved more successfully into partnership in a travel agency. He also launched the Bobby Charlton Sports Schools, running football coaching courses and camps for youngsters, and has been very active in football consultancy, work which took him to Africa in 1996 to help win votes in the Third World for Japan's World Cup bid. More recently he worked hard trying to win the 2006 World Cup for England, which eventually went to Germany.

Bobby Charlton always insisted that it would be the matches and medals he would want to talk about in later life to his children and friends, not the money, and he has remained in love with the game. In 1997 he marked his sixtieth birthday by playing a full ninety minutes in a match between a Salford Select XI and Moss Side Amateur Reserves.

'It was my birthday present to myself,' he declared, and one suspects that it was his favourite gift!

It's really a matter, though, of what he has given to us, as the late Geoffrey Green of *The Times* timelessly expressed it: 'It was the explosive facets of his play that will remain fresh in memory. His thinning fair hair streaming in the wind, he moved like a ship in full sail. He always possessed an elemental quality, jinking, changing feet and direction, turning gracefully on the ball, or accelerating through a gap surrendered by a confused enemy, he could be gone like the wind.'

That was Sir Bobby Charlton, who, looking back, tells me: 'When I first started with Manchester United the club won the FA Youth Cup five times in successive seasons. I think I played in three of the finals and Jimmy Murphy left us in no doubt about the importance of the youth programme. He used to say forget the League and the FA Cup, the youth team is the cream of the club.

'I remember I could hardly sleep the night before a youth match because I had been brainwashed by Jimmy into thinking it was the most important game of the season. In fact, in a way it was, because when Matt Busby started to have a few bad results he decimated the first team in the knowledge of what he had coming up behind. He didn't do things by halves and he said, "I'm bringing in the kids."

'That's how the Busby Babes came into being and we had a feeling that we were as good as anyone around in the world. They were great players who were on the verge of becoming world stars. This was an age before television but word was going round fast: "Look out for Manchester United".

'Then suddenly with the crash at Munich the whole thing had gone and the future for Manchester United was not as certain as it had seemed. Sir Matt Busby had to start all over again, which of course he did. He always stressed with his teams, both before and after Munich, that we were all good players and said that we must not be afraid to express ourselves.

'It was because of that that George Best felt he could beat six people in one run. It was why Denis Law would try acrobatic overhead kicks and why I would try to shoot for goal from such long distances, that a lot of the time was probably stupid, but which, I might add, also led to a few great goals.

'Then in 1968 we won the European Cup. I thought in the days before the final at Wembley that it was fate that we would win. We knew the Portuguese players, but we felt there was no way they were going to beat us. As soon as the match was won everyone went for Matt to pat him on the back and my feeling was that it was something for the lads who had died in the first attempt to become champions of Europe. It was a very emotional time.'

Chapter Twenty-five

SIMPLY THE BEST

——

I have always had difficulty trying to identify the real George Best.

On a football pitch he was such a many splendoured thing, but then there was the dark side that ultimately destroyed him at the age of fifty-nine. His whole life was a mass of contradictions. I remember the shy boy, the insecure lad almost tongue-tied when it came to being interviewed, and then watched him become a celebrity with the football world, as well as beauty queens, at his feet.

I often wanted to ask him, 'Would the real George Best please stand up' because while his talent as a player was constant and enduring he had a capricious restless nature that once away from the game made him totally unpredictable. Talk to ten different people about George Best and you could get ten different interpretations of his life and character.

He could be engaging and good company, but this is also the man who I spent two hours interviewing for a video and who then walked out of a dinner party thrown by the television company without so much as a goodbye, because he wanted a change of scene. And this was the man who, despite being the guest of honour, failed to turn up to a charity dinner to raise money for his own liver transplant fund, leaving a distraught wife in tears and the organisers able only to shrug and say, well, that's George.

And so it was, but the one inescapable conclusion about his life and work was that, despite all the let-downs, he was admired and loved, which was so evident at the end of his life. Two days after his death on 25 November 2005, when United played at West Ham, the London crowd burst into spontaneous applause during the intended one-minute's silence. At Old Trafford against West Bromwich Albion in the Carling Cup, the first home game after his death, the silence was observed because, as I was asked to explain to the crowd, 'We have lost someone close and we are still grieving.' The next match against Portsmouth three days later would be the time to applaud and celebrate his brilliance, I explained, which is exactly what they did.

At the West Bromwich match, Sir Alex Ferguson and visiting manager Bryan Robson laid wreaths beside a huge banner made by a group of fans that read: 'George simply the Best', and with posters bearing the face of George held aloft as the teams came out and during the silence, it was a very emotional and moving tribute.

The pavement opposite the Old Trafford ground was turned into a shrine with a floral carpet over a hundred yards long and studded with scarves, shirts, photographs and memorabilia put there by adoring fans representing not just United but many other clubs.

George had his well-documented troubles – his drinking and stormy personal life involving two marriages and countless relationships – but what came across in the days following his passing was a huge outpouring of love and affection, to match the respect and admiration everyone felt for him.

I am sure that people recognised that the person he hurt most by his behaviour was himself and so they forgave him. There are people who feel that he had a right to abuse his own liver, if that was his choice, but that he had no right to abuse someone else's following his life-saving transplant.

But even they realised that he was the one who suffered in the end, as those horrific photographs of him lying on his deathbed ravaged by illness showed only too vividly; it was hardly a peaceful passing. Maybe football supporters felt he couldn't help himself and they could understand that. The one thing that is clear is that there is a great love for George Best, as well as a fondness for his dazzling talents on the field of play, and it was a love still alive some forty years after his glory days.

Graham Williams, the Welsh international fullback who marked Best on his debut in 1963 against West Bromwich, was one of the guests at Old Trafford on the night United paid tribute to their fallen star and he captured the essence of George when he said: 'He would do his tricks and then he'd put his head down and his eyes would smile. Even if you won a tackle he would still smile.'

That was George, simply the Best, the man who despite the trials and tribulations put a smile on the face of football and left us with some very special memories. It stretches the imagination now to picture him at the start of his career, homesick and frightened when he first arrived at Old Trafford as a schoolboy. The landlady at his first digs, shared with David Sadler, described him as puny and petrified, looking more like a little jockey than a footballer. In fact he was so unhappy he went back home to Belfast with his pal, Eric McMordie. His dad, Dickie, and Matt Busby had to persuade him to give it another go.

But even though he still looked skinny and frail, he quickly made the youth team and then after only three reserve games, he was given his League debut against West Bromwich Albion at Old Trafford, just after turning seventeen, on 14 September 1963. He did well against Graham Williams my report at the time said, he had 'brightened up a dullish game' and it looked as if he was capable of brightening up a few more to come. As forecasts go, not bad!

He was dropped but returned to the first team at Christmas and from then on only injury or suspension kept him out of the team as he built up an incredible appearance record that would only waver when he began to lose interest in playing for Manchester United.

His first full season saw him make forty-one League appearances and score ten goals to help secure the 1965 Championship. He made a similar contribution the following season as United slipped to fourth, but that was more than made up for by the impact he made on Europe, with an extraordinary virtuoso display that destroyed Benfica in Lisbon, in the quarter-final of the European Cup.

The Reds had taken a narrow 3–2 lead to the Stadium of Light for the second leg and few of us thought it would be enough to see them through. Matt Busby's tactics were simply to play safe, especially in the opening stages, but after twenty minutes United had grabbed three goals, two of them from Best.

His second is my favourite of all time from any player. Harry Gregg punted his goal kick down the middle for David

Herd to flick on with a header. Best fastened on to the ball and weaved past three defenders, all on his own, to score a goal which was sensational by any standards. Even Eric Cantona didn't score one like that, nor Bobby Charlton, nor Denis Law, nor anyone else for that matter! United closed with an away second leg victory of 5–1 that gave George Best a world ranking. A bemused Busby could only say: 'When we made our plans, George must have had cotton wool stuffed in his ears!'

George stuck a souvenir sombrero on his head as we came off the plane back at Manchester Airport and the pictures went around the world. The man now dubbed 'El Beatle' had arrived on the world stage. United were immediately installed as favourites to go all the way and win the European Cup but they fell to Partizan Belgrade in the semi-finals. Significantly, Best had played the first leg with a sore knee and missed the return to undergo a cartilage operation. When George dropped out, the magic went with him.

United picked themselves up and won the Championship again the following season with George an ever-present and weighing in with his usual ten goals to qualify for another crack at Europe. George enjoyed his best-ever scoring year in 1967–68 with twenty-eight League goals from forty-one appearances and proved an inspiration in Europe, especially in the testing semi-final against mighty Real Madrid. He scored at Old Trafford for a 1–0 lead and then set up an aggregate winner in the second leg by scorching down the right wing to roll a pass into the path of Bill Foulkes who, for possibly the first time in his life, had left his defensive duties at centre half. Foulkes was a stranger up front but he made no mistake for a goal that brought United their destiny in the 1968 final of the European Cup against Benfica at Wembley.

Normal time ended with the game level at 1–1 and it wasn't looking good for Busby's boys, but once again George Best produced the inspired moment. Just a minute into extra time, he tore away to leave Cruz his marker trailing and then as Henrique came out he took the ball in a wide curve round the goalkeeper to clip it into an empty net. Benfica were broken and crashed 4–1, to give Matt Busby his dream.

George was voted Player of the Year in Northern Ireland. The English football writers gave him their award and six months later he was voted European Footballer of the Year, the youngest ever.

The following season, despite a great personal contribution from George of nineteen goals from forty-one League games, was the beginning of the end. Busby retired. Wilf McGuinness, Frank O'Farrell and finally Tommy Docherty took up the managerial reins but all found George increasingly difficult to manage.

He still had his magical moments and I will never forget the FA Cup fifth round at Northampton in February 1970. United won 8–2. George scored six and the manner he celebrated them – or rather didn't celebrate them – told you a lot about his character. After beating Kim Book the first time he briefly raised one arm in the air. After the others he simply walked back to the centre circle, no jumping about or signalling delight, as if to spare the luckless goalkeeper any further pain and embarrassment. George incidentally had just come back from a six-week suspension for that Cup tie and I had written in my preview that he should be given a run in the reserves rather than plunged straight back into first-team action. He certainly made nonsense of that opinion. I also enjoyed his hat trick against West Ham in a 4–2 win at Old Trafford in

September 1971, especially the moment he sold the great Bobby Moore a peach of a dummy.

But trouble was never far away as well and later that season pity the predicament of young manager McGuinness who caught Best in his hotel room with a girl a couple of hours before an FA Cup semi-final against Leeds United. The situation called for disciplinary action, but should you really leave your best player out of such a vitally important game? Wilf didn't, but they lost anyway.

Overall, though, George's behaviour didn't help team spirit, or as one team-mate told me: 'George thought he was the James Bond of soccer. He had everything he wanted, money, girls and tremendous publicity. He lived from day to day and until right to the end he got away with it. When he missed training or ran away, people made excuses for him. He didn't even have to bother to make them himself. He just didn't care.'

Inevitably in his final seasons there was trouble with referees and lengthening suspensions of six-week proportions. On one famous occasion Matt Busby arranged to meet him at Piccadilly Station in Manchester to accompany him to a disciplinary hearing at the FA in London. George failed to show. Matt waited for a couple of trains and then had to go to London on his own in support of a player who couldn't even be bothered to turn up for his own case. How embarrassing for the grand old man of football!

The player wouldn't have acted out of malice, just scattiness as he continued to live it up, highlighted by the story of the scruffy night porter who took champagne up to George's room in the early hours of one morning at his London hotel as he lay there on the bed surrounded by his casino winnings. Apparently not seeing Miss England there, the night porter asked him: 'Where did it all go wrong George?'

From George's point of view, he felt too much was being asked of him. He saw no serious attempt to strengthen the team being made, or as he put it: 'It was as if everyone thought that winning the European Cup was the end, but I was young and wanted more.'

So it all ended in tears as a disillusioned George slid down the slippery slope to play for Hibernian in Scotland, Dunstable, Stockport County, Fulham and in America, where incidentally he demonstrated his resilience by playing 150 games for three different clubs and scoring fifty-seven goals.

I wrote when he walked out of Manchester United for the last time in January 1974, after a 3–0 defeat against Queens Park Rangers: 'Slack Alice has got her man early!'

He was still only twenty-seven when he turned his back on Old Trafford to open a nightclub in Manchester and give it the randy name of Slack Alice. It was a typically defiant Best gesture and a reflection of his life at the time that centred a great deal on birds and booze. He was in the fast lane all right with a stunning girlfriend, Carolyn Moore, the reigning Miss Great Britain, on his arm when he decided he had had enough of Manchester United. As he put it himself after fleeing to Spain: 'Mentally and physically I am a bloody wreck.'

The rest of us found it hard to comprehend. Why should a young man who seemed to have everything want to throw it all away? I lambasted him in my newspaper reports, perhaps like many other people, dismayed that I would no longer have the pleasure of watching the most gifted and exhilarating player I have ever seen. But later I forgave him his early departure for a life with Slack Alice and her pals because, when you stood back, you realised George Best had paid his dues to the game. By the time he quit he had played 466 League, Cup and European games and scored 178 goals for United. Significantly also, once he had established himself in the side he rarely missed a game. In fact, in six of his seasons, when he was in full flow, he made 40, 41 or an ever-present 42 League appearances each year.

That's hardly the career of a fly-by-night and when you consider the knocks he took and the magic he so often created, he was entitled to call it a day when he felt he had had enough. In terms of entertainment he definitely packed in more than most. He transported so many of us to the heights of delight ... and I'm not even including the girls, who flocked to swoon at the feet of a cult figure who had led soccer into the Swinging Sixties.

George Best also won thirty-seven caps for Northern Ireland and scored nine goals without ever being in an Irish team good enough to put him on the big stage of a World Cup, a regret for football lovers, as well as for the man himself. He had his magic moments in international fixtures, though, one of them described by Nobby Stiles in his book, *After the Ball*, which expressed the brilliance of the man. It was Northern Ireland against England at Wembley with George already in his downward spiral and Nobby writes: 'George wasn't hugely in the picture in the first half and we came in at the interval a goal up. Then, early in the second half, I learned the extent of George Best's greatness, at a time when he was supposed to be heading for the gutter. Of course, I knew all about his brilliance. I'd seen him destroy Benfica in Lisbon's Stadium of Light. I'd seen him score goals after which you had to rub your eyes. I'd seen his talent erupt so many times in so many places, but never before had I been on the receiving end of the extraordinary action he could produce from, it seemed, nowhere. The Irish played a long ball over my head and as I turned to go for it, I was three or four yards ahead of George, but as we got to the edge of the box, George was a yard in front of me. He was bearing down on the goal and Banksy [Gordon Banks] was making himself as big as he could. But I knew Bestie so well, I could read clearly what he was going to do. He was going to fake a blasting shot and then drag it inside the goalkeeper, very tightly. So I had to make my tackle and I had to make it one of the best I had ever delivered. I went straight through the ball, and straight through George, but without the result I was looking for. I finished up on my back on the dead-ball line, looking back at George. He moved to his left past Banksy, and put the ball in the bottom of the net. Seventy five thousand fans who had an hour earlier booed and jeered the mere mention of his name filled the stadium with cheers. As I got to my feet I thought: "What a player." Afterwards I shook his hand and said: "Well done, George – only you could have done that. I'll never forget that goal." To me it summed up the career of Georgie Best. There he was, with the world falling in on his head, drinking, losing touch with what had made his name, but still able to produce something that made the little hairs on the back of your neck stand up.'

Chapter Twenty-six

DESTINY

That warm, humid night at Wembley was the moment so much came together for Manchester United. The time when the phoenix ascended to new heights, to look down on a football club honouring those of the family who had perished on the quest for European glory.

Sir Matt Busby and the other survivors of the Munich air crash could rest easy, their mission fulfilled as they celebrated a 4–1 victory over Benfica in the final of the European Cup on 29 May 1968. United had become the first English club to achieve the ultimate accolade. To win the championship of champions at any time is a marvellous achievement, but to do so a mere ten years after the Munich tragedy was little short of a football miracle.

Their holy grail had been captured and as Bobby Charlton and Bill Foulkes hugged Matt Busby at the end, you knew it was the fulfilment of their careers and that they were perhaps remembering comrades they had lost.

The preliminary round was hardly demanding, with Hibernians, a team of Maltese part-timers, beaten 4–0 on aggregate, but the first round proper put them up against Sarajevo. The Yugoslavs proved a tough team but United won the second leg at Old Trafford 2–1 following a goalless first game.

Górnik Zabrze, the dark horses who had knocked out Dynamo Kiev, were formidable opponents, too. In fact United lost 1–0 in Poland but came through on the strength of a 2–0 home win in the first leg.

So United went through for their fourth appearance in the European Cup semi-finals and a tie against much respected adversaries from their early days in Europe. In United's eyes, Real Madrid, under their great president Don Santiago Bernabeu, were the team which had set the standards and it just seemed appropriate that United should be meeting the club which had proved a step too far in their first season in European football in 1956.

The first leg was played at Old Trafford in front of a 63,000 crowd, full house, who constantly roared their side forward. Indeed, United supplied most of the attacking play but, for all their possession, could do no more than force a 1–0 win with the goal from George Best. The Spaniards, so well versed in the art of two-legged ties in Europe, seemed quietly confident about overhauling Manchester United's slender lead in Madrid. Their optimism seemed quite justified as they went into a 2–0 lead and then, after United had pulled a goal back, increased their advantage to go off at half time 3–1 up.

But as Busby explained later: 'Although we were 3–1 down on the night I reminded the players that the aggregate score was 3–2 and that we were in fact only one goal down. I told them simply to go out and play.' And this is what his team did and with such flair and force that the Spanish champions crumbled and lost their grip on the game. With attack once more at the forefront of their tactics, United were a different proposition. David Sadler left his defensive duties and started to advance upfield to such telling effect that in the seventieth minute he was on hand to turn in a header from George Best, following Pat Crerand's free kick.

Level now on aggregate, United had their tails up and just five minutes later they stunned Real with a goal courtesy of the player least likely to score. As Pat Crerand said: 'Bill Foulkes of all people – goodness knows what he was doing so far upfield. All I know is that people have talked about providence and about fate evening things out after Munich ten years previously.'

United had become the first English club to reach the final of the European Cup and take Matt Busby even closer to his dream of conquering Europe. The European Cup was finally won as much by character as ability. Matt Busby described it as heart, the kind of fighting spirit that his team had shown to pull the game out of the fire in Madrid.

It was hard going against the Portuguese champions with tension seeming to cramp the style of both teams. Perhaps because the match was being played on home soil, United were the first to settle and establish themselves as the team taking the game to their opponents.

Crucial duels were taking place all over the field. Bill Foulkes knew it was imperative for him to win the aerial battle with the towering Torres and Nobby Stiles was certainly aware that his marking of the elusive Eusebio was critical. Benfica also knew they had particular players to mark and the rugged Cruz became George Best's watchdog, several times bringing him down without hesitation. When

Cruz missed him on one occasion Humberto sailed in and was booked.

United's persistence in attack took a long time to find a chink in the visitors' defence, but in the fifty-third minute David Sadler crossed from a deep position on the left. Bobby Charlton attacked the ball, glancing it over the goalkeeper into the far corner of the net. That was the signal for Benfica to throw caution to the wind to step up their own forward momentum and draw on the experience garnered from playing in five European Cup finals. Nine minutes from the end they pulled level through a finely worked goal. Augusto put the ball in for Torres to nod down. Eusebio made a run which drew the defence and it was Jaime Graca who latched on to the ball and scored with a fierce shot from a narrow angle.

This was the moment when United dug deep. Benfica stepped up the pressure and twice Eusebio broke through to test Alex Stepney. His second effort brought him face to face with the United goalkeeper and he unleashed a rocket which Stepney saved with such effect that even his opponent applauded!

United were faltering and as Stiles put it to me later: 'If the game had had another ten minutes without a break I think we would have lost. We suddenly realised how tired we were. For me it was like the World Cup final all over again when Germany pulled level just before the end. It came close to knocking the heart out of us.' But there was still something there and when the whistle came for the completion of normal time, Busby seized his chance to inspire his players for a renewed effort.

'I told them they were throwing the game away with careless passing and hitting the ball anywhere. I said they must keep possession and start to play their football again,' he explained.

Although Eusebio was always a threat, Nobby Stiles came out on top in his fourth game against the Portuguese star – three for United and one for England – and what's more he played him cleanly. 'One newspaper said Eusebio had asked for more protection from the referee but I don't believe he ever said it. I never went out to kick him. I respected him and found him all right,' said Stiles.

Extra time opened dramatically as United, with Busby's wise words heeded, swept forward and scored twice in two minutes. In only the third minute Brian Kidd headed on Alex Stepney's clearance to Best who immediately homed in on goal. He took the ball round the defenders in a splendidly curving arc and then past the goalkeeper before popping it into the empty net.

It was Best at his best and Kidd was quick to match him with a goal to mark his nineteenth birthday. Kidd whipped in a close-range header which was blocked by Henrique, but as the ball came out the youngster got in a second header which this time looped over the goalkeeper. Kidd then laid on a goal for Bobby Charlton and United sailed home with a 4–1 victory.

Brian Kidd, the babe of the side, said: 'I honestly felt it was something that was meant to be. We knew we had to do it, if only for Sir Matt Busby. My moment of glory came with my goal to mark my nineteenth birthday, the treasured moment I will never forget.'

Bobby Charlton, unashamedly in tears at the end of the game, said: 'My thoughts on the day were that we just wouldn't lose. I can remember thinking that we had come too far and had been through too much for us to fail in that final match.

'I knew it would be hard work, but I also knew that we would find something extra. That's something British teams have always had, this resilience, especially in extra time. This is what England had produced to win the World Cup two years previously. It was in the nick of time. Without being disrespectful to the players involved, the 1968 team was probably no longer at its best. We had faded in the League to let Manchester City win the title and a lot of us were past our peak. I knew I for one wasn't going to get another chance and about half the team were in the same boat.

'So we were all pretty determined and, as I say, defeat was never in our minds. Our first goal confirmed that idea because I scored it with a header – and that didn't happen very often! When the final whistle went I remember thinking that it was the ultimate achievement, not just for the players but for the club and Sir Matt Busby. I suppose I can't speak for everyone, but I think I probably do, when I say that we felt winning the European Cup had been a duty to Manchester United. For some of us it had become a family thing. We had been together so long.

'Nobby Stiles was an important cog in that team, too. He used to tidy up for us. He seemed able to sense trouble and where danger was going to come from. So he was always there ready and waiting, a great reader of the game. He was a bit like a sheepdog keeping everything under control. If one of the sheep tried to break away, he would dart into action and put the breakaway back in the pen.

'Johnny Aston had a particularly good game in the final, running the legs off their fullback down his wing to produce some great crosses, while at the same time he was pulling their defence wide, which gave the rest of us more room.'

The teams that night were:

Manchester United: STEPNEY, BRENNAN, DUNNE, CRERAND, FOULKES, STILES, BEST, KIDD, CHARLTON, SADLER, ASTON. SUB: RIMMER.

Benfica: JOSE HENRIQUE, ADOLFO, HUMBERTO, JACINTO, CRUZ, JAIME GRACA, COLUNA, JOSE AUGUSTO, TORRES, EUSEBIO, SIMOES. SUB: NASIMENTO.

Chapter Twenty-seven

HE HAD A DREAM

All the sixties legends, bar the injured Denis Law, played in the final of the European Cup, but the man who stole the show came from the shadows.

It is harsh to describe John Aston junior in those terms because he was a top-class footballer and a model professional, but regrettably that is how he was perceived by a great many supporters: there to make up the numbers rather than weave the kind of magic supplied by the superstars.

They were not slow to express their impatience and groan if things didn't go right for a youngster who had joined the club from school and worked his way through the junior and reserve sides. Normally when a local boy breaks through at Old Trafford the crowd will back him and encourage him, but John was unhappily an exception; perhaps the fans were suspicious in John's case because his dad, a great United player in his day, was also a coach at Old Trafford.

Certainly he suffered by comparison with the great players who surrounded him, rather in the way that David Herd's magnificent marksmanship was invariably overshadowed when put alongside the exploits of Charlton, Law and Best. So John Aston always seemed to have something to prove and he believes he was judged by the demanding standards of his time.

'My problem was that I was young and in a team with three genuine world-class players. If you picked a world eleven these days you wouldn't pick three from Manchester United, but in my day you would have picked Law, Best and Charlton. For me, it was a bit like being a workhorse alongside thoroughbreds. It did get to me, but my reaction was a stiff upper lip. I just used to grit my teeth and say, "To Hell with it, let's get on with it."'

Aston reckons he didn't get much help from his manager either.

'Matt Busby was a hard-bitten, uncompromising man who had to make some tough decisions, but he was a manager, what else do you expect? He was never a father figure to me. I had these tremendous problems with the crowd and never once did he offer to help me. I accepted it. That's the way the club was run. It worked on a star system. He got what he considered to be the best players and he put you in the side and you performed or you didn't. To put it another way, he taught you to swim three or four strokes and then threw you in at the deep end. You sank or swam.'

But on the night of the European Cup final, the under-appreciated John Aston was, by common consent, man of the match. He was in the deep end, but as he puts it himself: 'I was one of those who did several lengths that night at Wembley.'

George Best won plaudits for his pivotal goal in extra time, Bobby Charlton was rightly proud of scoring with a header and in fact every one in the team rose to the occasion with splendid displays, but none more so than the young left winger. He was electric down his wing, a blur of blue that devastated Adolfo, the Benfica right back.

With typical modesty John describes his performance: 'The lad was a decent right back but he had no pace, so I was on a winner from the start.'

I put it to John recently that it must have been very satisfying during the game knowing that he was playing out of his skin after all the stick he had taken from the crowd, but he insists the thought never entered his mind.

'You see it had always been my dream to play in the final of the European Cup and here I was, actually living the dream. So I didn't have room for any other thoughts other than enjoying my game,' he explained.

Even afterwards he puts the emphasis more on the significance of victory for the club, rather than seeing it as his own personal redemption.

'It is one of the few things in my life that never diminishes with time. I remember the George Best goal, a great Alex Stepney save and I can remember playing well. But they were all very secondary to what it all meant. It was Matt Busby and Manchester United's greatest night. That's what makes me very proud. When Munich happened I was ten. I played with lads later on who were in that crash. My life had doubled by then but for people like Bill Foulkes and Bobby Charlton it must have gone by in a flash. I had no idea at the time of the magnitude of what the club and those players had achieved and what it had meant to them.'

In my view John Aston was always worth much more than that one European performance at Wembley, outstanding though it was. He had for instance made twenty-six appearances, scoring five goals, to help win the Championship that qualified the team for Europe and in the run-up to meeting Benfica at Wembley he had contributed ten League goals from thirty-four appearances, a useful contribution.

You would have hoped that his European success would have triggered a more popular run with the fans but it never seemed to happen, a situation not helped by a broken leg the following season which prevented him from climbing the heights again. In 1972, having amassed a career record of 164 appearances in all competitions and twenty-seven goals, he was transferred to Luton Town for £30,000.

He later played for Mansfield and Blackburn but North Manchester was always his home and after football he joined the family's pet food business.

One of the players John impressed in his United days was the England international whose place he took in the first team, John Connelly, signed from Burnley in 1964 for £60,000.

Says Connelly: 'As John was a winger like myself I took a keen interest in him. He was a speedy winger who used his pace to great effect and he was a good crosser of the ball, as well as being a brave player. I don't think we played together in the same team many times and John basically took my place when I left. I had moved on by the time United played in the final of the European Cup when he probably had his best game. I watched it on television and remember thinking what a magnificent game he had. Benfica couldn't handle his pace and it was great that he enjoyed his finest hour on one of the biggest nights in the club's history. It couldn't have happened to a more level-headed lad.'

It's perhaps difficult to describe John Aston as one of Manchester United's legends, but he certainly turned in a legendary performance that night against Benfica. Similarly it's stretching things to include John Connelly in the list of all-time greats because he was only at Old Trafford for two years.

But nothing can detract from the tremendous impact he made, winning a Championship medal in his first season as an ever-present on the right wing and scoring fifteen goals in a high-scoring attack. It was an attack described by Nobby Stiles as one 'dripping with goals'!

He did well enough the following season, too, including scoring a hat trick in a European Cup match, but his goals dried up and with Aston on the horizon he was soon on his way to Blackburn and Bury. He won twenty England caps and scored seven goals for the international team in a career that saw him make a total of nearly 600 League appearances.

He retired in 1972 after opening a fish and chip shop near Burnley, and says: 'I always look for United's result first, and I keep in touch through the Former Players Association. I enjoyed my career. Some of the lads want to finish at the top and won't go down the divisions, but it gave me a lot of satisfaction to pass things on to younger players. I liked it at Bury, even if I did have more managers there than I had in the rest of my career!'

With many fans blinded by the shimmering skills of the glamour players and failing to look for the all-important team players who bind the soloists together, David Sadler was another player who perhaps didn't get the accolades he deserved. David was a sportsman who could turn his hand to any athletic activity and could play in just about every position in a football team. It was this versatility, priceless for Matt Busby and his other managers, which in the long term proved damaging to his career. Not that you could get any hostile reaction from the man himself, genial, laid-back and still devoting tremendous time and effort to the Manchester United cause as a founder member of the Association of Former Manchester United Players and still their efficient secretary. Now he is the team player who holds the old boys together. In the sixties he undoubtedly sacrificed himself for the good of the team, playing in so many different positions that he failed to nail down one particular role until too late in the day.

He was an England amateur international at the age of sixteen and it was as a centre forward that he first came to notice playing with Maidstone United. Indeed, after joining United as an amateur (and retaining that status for three months so that he could further his international amateur career) he played at centre forward in the team that won the FA Youth Cup of 1964, scoring a hat trick in the final against Swindon Town.

He won promotion to the first team in various forward positions, but Busby and Jimmy Murphy also saw him as a capable deputy in midfield and defence, which didn't particularly please him at the time.

'I didn't want to become a "basher" which playing centre half can sometimes make you, but I still became a jack of all trades and in our League Championship success of 1964, I played in three different positions. The following season saw me wearing five different shirt numbers,' he explained.

He had been an ever-present in the European campaign, again demonstrating his adaptability by standing in at different times for Bill Foulkes at centre half, Nobby Stiles as the defensive wing half and up front for Denis Law. He was certainly a key figure in the final, moving from defence into a more attacking role in midfield for the extra time period, a move that undoubtedly tipped the balance of the game in United's favour. He gave the midfield an added momentum that stepped up the intensity of the attack to produce three United goals in the final half hour.

Eventually he settled into what he now considers his best position, playing at centre back alongside the centre half. It was in this position that he won his four England caps and I believe that if he had been allowed to specialise there earlier in his career he might have won many more.

But if the fans didn't always appreciate his team qualities his team-mates certainly did. This is how Nobby Stiles rates him: 'When we won the European Cup I got all the credit for looking after Eusebio, for keeping the great Portuguese marksman quiet, but actually the man who deserved a lot of the praise was David Sadler. David was best known as a centre forward early in his career and then later as a centre half, but that night at Wembley he turned out in midfield, a job he did with typical efficiency.

'He was never a flashy sort of performer, playing his football efficiently, skilfully and with great composure and a lot of people tended to underestimate his contribution. Not his team-mates, though. We all thought the world of what he brought to the team, his versatility and unselfishness. It was valuable to have a player who could do so well in so many positions.

'The Eusebio situation was typical. I had faced him for United in 1965 and England in 1966 and people just assumed that I was policing him again in 1968. Some of the time I did, but I wasn't in midfield for United as I was for England. Instead I played alongside Bill Foulkes at the back and the idea was that David would track when he was deep so that I wouldn't be pulled out of position. David worked really hard on a hot, draining night, running all over the pitch, but I got all the pats on the back.

'Of course that didn't bother David, who is a lovely, modest fellow. We used to call him the "Quiet Man" after the John Wayne film. He was very much an unsung hero, chronically underrated for such a fine all-round footballer. It seemed that the world at large just didn't realise how good he was.

'I honestly believe he deserved more caps for England. He was so unlucky in 1970 when he was part of the party of twenty-eight players taken to Mexico for the World Cup finals, but one of the half a dozen who were trimmed from the squad before the tournament started.

'He always had a lovely, level temperament, on and off the park. Then as now, he was always willing to oblige anyone and he has played a leading part in making our Association of former players such a success.

'David was an eternal link man at Wembley against Benfica and he still is now. Doing so much to keep us all together. A lot of people who didn't really know David Sadler didn't fully appreciate him.

'But I did.'

The babe of the team, Brian Kidd, was sensitive to the Busby legacy after Munich because he was another of the boys like Nobby Stiles from St Patrick's, a school with a great reputation for producing footballers in Collyhurst, an inner-city area to the east of Manchester.

He was only nine at the time of the crash but he had shared in the sorrow and was delighted to join Old Trafford from school. He burst on to the first-team scene after showing up well on a tour of Australia in the summer of 1967 and he had won a regular place up front by the time of the European Cup final.

Like George Best he seemed to lose his way a little after the retirement of Busby, and I recall him complaining as one of the younger people in the squad that there seemed to be one rule for the stars and one for the others. He didn't suit Tommy Docherty who sold him to Arsenal for £110,000 in August 1974. Two years later he moved back up north to join Manchester City before playing also for Everton, Bolton and then several teams in America.

He joined the managerial merry-go-round with Barrow, Swindon and Preston before Alex Ferguson brought him back to Old Trafford to work on the football in the community project, later promoting him to set up a new scouting and coaching system. He became assistant manager when Archie Knox left to join Glasgow Rangers but eventually fell out with the United manager and became manager of Blackburn, only to quit after relegation. The FA took him on board as a coach with England but he returned to club football with Leeds United as first the youth coach and later the first-team coach.

Prostate cancer saw him drop out of football for a while, but he is now fully recovered, fit and at the time of writing looking for a job back in the game.

Chapter Twenty-eight

EL BANDIDO

———

Nobby Stiles certainly belongs in the panoply of legends. Even the mums loved him after his dance of joy as he jigged his way round Wembley, socks round his ankles, to celebrate England's World Cup victory in 1966. It was a brilliant achievement for a player who had started out pint-sized and short-sighted but ended up a World and European Cup winner.

His career was packed with tribulations as well as triumphs as a reputation for fearless football and a determination to get stuck in went before him. It was his experience in South America (when he went with United as European champions to play Estudiantes for the World Club Championship in September 1968) that gives me my favourite memory of the player dubbed by his team-mates as the 'Toothless Tiger': because he was missing his top front teeth and he was a tiger in the tackle.

The Argentinians knew all about him when we arrived in Buenos Aires, but Nobby was shocked to discover that the newspapers had reported Estudiantes' manager Otto Gloria as saying that Nobby Stiles was 'an assassin' and Estudiantes even ran an article in their match programme by the Benfica chief, calling Stiles 'brutal, badly intentioned and a bad sportsman.'

Stiles of course had been in the England team which had beaten Argentina in 1966 when Sir Alf Ramsey had described their team as 'animals' and he was the focus and hate target for the Estudiantes supporters who knew all about his reputation for tough tackling and had seen it in the England match against their country. The hostility for Stiles actually started as he walked off the plane in Buenos Aires and an excitable commentator was announcing the arrival of the United players over the loudspeaker system as they walked through the airport.

'Bobby Charlton ... El Supremo', he shouted. 'George Best ... El Beatle', he declared. Then his voice went up an octave and there was a great answering roar as he went on: 'Nobby Stiles ... El Bandido!'

That game in South America in many ways summed up his career. Who else could be head-butted by an opponent destined to become the manager of a World Cup-winning team? Yet, that was what Carlos Bilardo, an aggressive young man before managing Argentina to their World Cup success in Mexico in 1986, did to Nobby in the first leg in Buenos Aires.

Says Stiles: 'That was bad enough, but Bilardo then threw himself down as if it was me who had hit him. I think the referee was going to send me off, but I was able to point to the blood running from a cut eye and it made him change his mind.'

The referee caught up with Nobby in the second half, though, when a linesman flagged against him for offside.

'I didn't think I was off and I just threw my arm in the air.

The referee sent me off for dissent. I was pig-sick. There was a lot going on in the game and it seemed silly that I was sent off for waving my arm.

'Mind you, the referee was a funny chap. He was smoking a cigarette when we all came down the tunnel to go out on the pitch. A lot of people smoke but you don't expect to see the referee having a puff like that.

'I suppose before the game had even started I was regarded as the villain of the piece. I knew I always had a reputation as a fairly aggressive player, but the South American press had really gone to town.

'Then I remember coming out of the stadium after the match to get on our coach. It was dark and shadowy when I suddenly felt something thrust into my back with a voice whispering into my ear: "Now then El Bandido". I thought my end had come – until I realised it was Brian Kidd!'

Conigliaro gave Estudiantes a 1–0 win with Busby saying: 'They crucified Nobby Stiles but I was extremely proud of the way the boys accepted every provocation with hardly a murmur.' Stiles was of course banned for the return leg at Old Trafford. Willie Morgan scored for a 1–1 draw but they lost on aggregate thanks to the defeat in South America.

The image of Nobby as an all-action controversial player wouldn't have suited him when he first joined United from school, when his peers looked at him in such disbelief that Jimmy Murphy felt it necessary to tell the other boys: 'Don't worry about Nobby. He's a Collyhurst lad. They breed great boxers and footballers there. He can take care of himself.'

Soon his contemporaries discovered what Jimmy had meant, as Nobby, never a cultured player, became a World Cup winner with England as well as a European Cup winner with

Manchester United, a distinction only he and Bobby Charlton hold. Charlton said: 'As a midfield player with United I used to turn round and see Nobby behind me and think, "We're OK." It was the same playing for England, particularly if the opposition had someone a bit hard playing for them. I was always glad Nobby was on our side.'

But for all his success, life has not been easy for this son of an undertaker raised in modest circumstances in downtown Collyhurst. There have been as many downs as ups and in many respects his whole life has been a battle, as indeed it is for most footballers striving to make the grade as a professional, but in his case there were several additional hurdles to surmount.

Being born in a cellar during an air raid on Manchester during the Second World War seemed like an omen for a toddler who was knocked down by a bus. He got up from that, but more serious for an ambitious sportsman was poor eyesight, a problem that Nobby says came to a head in a match against Everton at Goodison Park.

'I went to receive a throw-in from the wing half and I suddenly realised I was guessing when it came to timing the ball and to where and to whom I was going to play it. I was given a man to mark and in the flow of play I frequently lost sight of him. It was a terrible shock but, perhaps out of fear of what I would be told if I raised the issue with Matt Busby, I kept quiet.'

It was Harry Gregg who came to his rescue, after noting his struggle to see properly when they were playing cards. He went to see Busby and said: 'You know, Boss, you just have to do something about Nobby's eyesight. The kid is really struggling. He's putting down the wrong cards. He just can't read them. We just have to imagine how it's affecting his play.'

The club finally sorted him out and so began the trademark big black specs and the ritual of contact lenses for training and playing. It brought a marked improvement in his football, though his new look evidently didn't impress England colleague Jack Charlton.

Nobby tells the story in his book *After the Ball*: 'It was in the dressing room before playing for the Football League that I first met Jack Charlton. We eyed each other across the room and I was not thrilled when, referring to my contact lenses, he recalled to the world his first impression of me. He said he saw this "little Japanese-looking bastard fitting these bloody great things into his eyes".'

Despite the eyesight problem Nobby's career took off, though he was still dogged by controversy, such as the time he flattened Jacky Simon playing against France on the road to the 1966 World Cup final.

Nobby describes it: 'I remember the tackle well enough. It was the one from hell, which is exactly where it threatened to put me. As I recall the build-up, we were attacking along the right with George Cohen on the ball and Simon, a very good player, tracking him. When the French goalkeeper, Marcel Aubour, gathered up the ball and threw it out to his team-mate, I was already on the move, watching the ball looping down and lining up my tackle.

'Maybe I should say what was in my mind as I went into the tackle, that would create such a storm of headlines and criticism. It was to hit the ball – and him – just as he turned. It is not a foul if you go through the ball, hitting it with all the force you have and that takes you through the player. That is a hard but legal tackle and that was my ambition. The objective is not to hurt the player but to remind him of the force of body contact in the game, to announce your presence so that the next time you are in his vicinity, he will think twice about doing something fancy, and possibly dangerous, with the ball.

'What went wrong was that while I was following an old instruction of Matt Busby's, who always used to say, "Norrie, let him know you are there in the first five minutes", the ball had gone. Simon, the playmaker, who liked to stroke it around, had on this occasion whipped the ball away at first contact. That compounded my mistiming, making the tackle look even more horribly late. The crowd shrieked and although the referee, Arturo Yamaski, a Peruvian, took no action, a FIFA observer in the stand did. He booked me and took me within an inch of being banished from the World Cup.'

The Football Association wanted Nobby out of the team for the next game against Argentina, already a powder-keg clash, but Alf Ramsey stood by his man and told the FA that if Nobby went, so did he!

As Nobby puts it: 'When I was being hung, drawn and quartered by the press, the television panellists and the high-ups in the Football Association and the world ruling body FIFA wanted me thrown out of the tournament, that was when Alf stood up for me against a world that suddenly seemed very hostile indeed and when I became indebted to him for the rest of my life.'

It was yet another stormy chapter in a career that had seen him hit on the head by a bottle in Madrid, hissed and spat at in Italy and described as an assassin in Buenos Aires.

United missed him, though, when he left in 1971 after eleven years of first-team football that saw him make over 300 League appearances and win twenty-eight caps for England. A succession of knee injuries and two cartilage operations had perhaps slowed him down a little, but typically he was far from finished. He joined Middlesbrough for £20,000 and on his first return to Old Trafford was given the kind of hero's welcome afforded to few players in new colours. But he was always the fans' favourite. After two years at Ayrsome Park he spent eight seasons with Preston North End, the first as a player, three as a coach and then four as manager.

He had a spell in Canada with Vancouver Whitecaps as coach working for John Giles, his brother-in-law, who was the manager. He followed John to assist him as youth coach at West Bromwich Albion and later returned to Old Trafford to work for Alex Ferguson in a similar capacity, as well as joining the after-dinner speaking circuit.

On the eve of the 2002 World Cup he suffered a heart attack. Still living in Manchester, he has made a full recovery and says now: 'It was maybe a signal for the enjoyment of the rest of my days. A man couldn't have had a better wife or sons or friends, or memories of the one thing that had coloured all his days, the game of football, the great passion of the blood in my part of the town.'

And he didn't do badly either, or as he puts it himself: 'I thought of how I'd come to win a World Cup and a European Cup medal even though I was born a half-blind dwarf who was bombed by the Germans and run over by a trolley bus before he was one.'

Chapter Twenty-nine

BIG AL

There was certainly no doubting the high esteem in which Alex Stepney was held by his peers, always a major personality in the dressing room as well as a commanding figure in goal.

In fact when I once asked Matt Busby for the decisive factor that enabled him to turn a team stunned by defeat in the semi-finals of the European Cup in 1966 into champions in 1968, he didn't hesitate: signing Alex Stepney was his instant response.

Busby said: 'I only saw him play once for Millwall but it was enough. I kept the picture at the back of my mind so that when I decided we needed a new goalkeeper I knew he was the man. He was the final piece in the jigsaw.'

Like many new players Alex took time to settle but by the end of his first full season he had knocked fourteen goals off the total conceded by the Reds the previous year. Clean sheets had become quite regular and once again United had a goalkeeper to measure up to the standard set by Harry Gregg. Tommy Docherty would later say: 'Alex had more clean sheets than a laundry.'

In terms of Europe 'Big Al', as he was called by his team-mates, had bought an ageing side time. They had blown their big chance in 1966 when they lost to Partizan Belgrade and the team was getting a little long in the tooth. It was essential they qualified quickly for the European Cup again, before it was too late for the likes of Bobby Charlton, Pat Crerand and Denis Law.

So Matt Busby made his key move and brought Stepney from Chelsea in September 1966 and with the Londoner behind them in goal, they won the League with a flourish, memorably beating West Ham 6–1 at Upton Park in the penultimate game of the season.

The Reds were back in Europe and this time they made no mistake, beating Benfica in the final, with Stepney emerging a hero with his inspiring save from Eusebio.

Despite never going back to London after signing for United (he still lives in the Rochdale area) there is no doubting his Southern origins, as you would imagine of a player born at Mitcham in Surrey, who started his football in the amateur ranks of Tooting and Mitcham, before being snapped up by Millwall. He was still a long way from European glory, though, when Millwall were relegated to the Fourth Division in 1964, but their slim, lithe goalkeeper helped launch a revival which saw the Londoners bounce back at the first attempt and then move into the Second Division.

Despite still being out of the top flight his talent stood out and he was called up for three England Under 23 appearances. He also caught the attention of Tommy Docherty, then the manager of Chelsea, who signed him for a record fee for a goalkeeper of £50,000. However, the Doc had only signed him as insurance cover for an unsettled Peter Bonetti. Once Bonetti had made up his mind that he wanted to stay, Alex became available and after only four months, in which he made just one League appearance, he was on his way to join United.

Busby put him straight into the team in mid-September, to succeed Harry Gregg and David Gaskell, and watched his team race away in the League and conquer Europe the following year. As Sir Matt said at the time: 'I thought, as Eusebio raced towards him, that all my dreams of winning the European Cup were going to be shattered again. He shot with all his power but Alex held it.'

In typical modest and offhand style, the player puts it: 'I think the save stands out in people's minds because of the time of it in the game, near the end with the score at 1–1. Actually he hit it straight at me. He did hit it hard but I remember standing there holding the ball and thinking: "Thank you."'

The save was, nevertheless, the pivotal point of the match.

In twelve seasons at Old Trafford, Stepney made 433 League appearances and played in another hundred cup games. He also achieved the rare distinction for a goalkeeper of scoring two League goals ... called up in the relegation season of 1973–74 to score with two penalties.

Although chosen twenty times as a substitute for England, Sir Alf Ramsey gave him his only full cap against Sweden at Wembley just one week before he was to play there again in the European Cup final. Alex likes to say: 'Perhaps he did it to give me the feel of Wembley ready for the European game.'

The lack of caps was undoubtedly due to the presence of rivals in his era of the calibre of Gordon Banks and Peter Bonetti, though we can all wonder about the outcome against Germany in the World Cup defeat in Mexico in 1970, had it been Stepney taking over from the sick Banks rather than Bonetti, who seemed overcome by the occasion.

It was the kind of high-pressure situation that would have left the unflappable and steady Stepney absolutely unfazed.

After a fine career for United, he left at the end of season 1977–78 to play for Dallas Tornado in the States. He had a spell with Altrincham on his return and later scouted for Southampton and Exeter City. He also did commercial work for Stockport County and Rochdale, as well as running a pub.

Always popular with United's fans, it's a testimony to their respect for him that they ignored the fact that for six years, until the departure of Joe Royle as manager at Maine Road, he was the specialist goalkeeping coach of deadly rivals Manchester City! More recently he has worked in a similar capacity on a part-time basis at Burnley. Now he seems to have come back home to Old Trafford for good as a familiar face on the club's television screens.

Any discussion of United's defence in Alex Stepney's era has got to lead to Tony Dunne and it is typical that I have only arrived at the left back position towards the end of the Busby legends. I say typically because Tony was the essential quiet man of the team, self-effacing, publicity shy and easy to over-look in any review of the strength of the swashbuckling side of the sixties.

Yet, the modest Irishman, recruited from Shelbourne in 1960 for an almost nominal fee of £5,000, played 414 League games for United and made fifty-four FA Cup appearances in addition to playing in forty European ties.

I have no hesitation including him in my roll call of legends because this was a player who signalled the arrival of the small, speedy attacking fullback to replace the old-style rufty-tufty defender. Tony was certainly fast and contributed hugely to United's sixties success.

He won thirty-three caps for the Republic of Ireland (and was voted Irish Footballer of the Year in 1969) but even internationally he seemed to play second fiddle to the more famous players. The fact was he was a players' player, but I think the lack of appreciation away from the dressing room sometimes rankled with him. I recall being on a Continental tour with United one pre-season when he pointed out to me a poster at our hotel, advertising the match the club had come to play.

It read: 'Manchester United with Bobby Charlton, George Best and Denis Law etc.' He told me it was nice to be listed on the poster for a change. I looked but couldn't see his name until he said: 'Yes, there I am ... Etcetera Dunne.'

It was the story of his life. He just didn't make the headlines because his career ran so smoothly, with consistent form, little injury and he was never in trouble on or off the field. Scoring was never going to project him as a match-winner either, with only two goals in thirteen years of first-team football.

Like a lot of 'Steady Eddies', he tended to be taken for granted and Tommy Docherty let him move to Bolton in 1973. There was still plenty of football left in him, though, and he went on to play nearly 200 games for the Burnden Park club.

After Bolton he played briefly in America before returning to Bolton as a coach. He also coached in Norway but eventually settled back in Manchester.

Of course, there have always been low-profile players at Old Trafford who don't quite make it as legends. Don't underestimate their contribution, though. I am thinking of Pat Dunne, a delightful Irishman picked up from Shamrock Rovers for £10,500 and given a debut in September 1964, in place of David Gaskell. It was as if he came from nowhere and went back almost as quickly. Having made just a handful of appearances the following season, Pat went home to Dublin, via Plymouth Argyle. But for that one season in 1964–65 he was quite legendary in terms of his title contribution, in a remarkable, but brief, flirtation with glory.

And at least he left with a Championship medal, which made him a lot more fortunate than Francis Burns, who played in every round of the 1968 European Cup triumph, only to be dropped for the final. He did leave with a warm memory, though, as he told me on a trip back to Manchester from Australia where he now lives.

'I appeared in every round, playing in either the home or away leg including the semi-final tie against Real Madrid at Old Trafford. But with Shay Brennan returning after injury I missed out on the final. Naturally I was devastated and Nobby Stiles could see it as we sat in the dressing room at Wembley after beating Benfica. Without hesitating he came across and gave me his number six shirt and said it would perhaps make up for not being presented with a medal. Actually, the club later made a medal for those of us who had played in the earlier rounds, but had missed the final. Nothing can take anything away from Nobby's gesture of offering me his Cup shirt, though.'

Francis, who lost all his knee cartilages through injuries that restricted him to just over one hundred League games for United, still has the treasured shirt and brought it with him from Australia a few years ago, for a reunion of the Cup-winning team.

'For some reason the name of Alex Stepney was missing when the rest of the lads signed Nobby's jersey for me, but I have been to see him and they are all there now.'

At least a legendary moment!

Chapter Thirty

A GIANT OF A MAN

———

So we have walked the walk and met the legends who are woven into the history of Manchester United in the time of Sir Matt Busby, and it is only fitting that we should finish where we started, with the man who became a legend in his own lifetime.

Honoured and fêted at the end of his twenty-five years at the helm, he had woken and then steered the sleeping giant to the ultimate triumph in Europe. I shall never forget the day when the city fathers rightly made him a Freeman of Manchester, an occasion that inspired him to allow us a rare insight into his approach to life and sport.

The mud of the training ground and the clamour of a match seemed far removed as he stood in the Town Hall, with a red carnation jauntily in his buttonhole, looking immaculate in white tie and tails with the silver insignia of a Commander of the British Empire tucked snugly round his neck.

All day, the flag of Manchester United had flown from the top of the Town Hall to greet Manchester's first Freeman from the world of sport and the city's sixty-sixth member of this distinguished company.

Inside that evening, the sombre stone walls seemed to take on the man's warmth as he accepted his honour and sketched his humble birth in a pitman's cottage in Scotland. He told us of the delayed visa that had prevented him from going to America. 'I emigrated to Manchester instead,' he said.

Then he described his anxious days struggling to make his mark with Manchester City and his move to Liverpool before becoming the manager of Manchester United at the end of the war. This was the moment when he chose to reveal his deep love and feeling for football behind the honours and trophies.

'I won't deny that it is pleasant to succeed in what you strive to do, but winning football matches at all costs is not the test of true achievement. There is nothing wrong with trying to win, as long as you don't set the garland and the prize above the game. There is no dishonour in defeat, as long as you play to the limit of your strength and skill,' he said.

'If the game is not always played in that spirit it is unfortunate and there have been incidents, much publicised, which have brought no credit to the game. I think therefore, that I should say that what matters above all things is that the game should be played in the right spirit, with the utmost resource of skill and courage, with fair play and no favour, with every man playing as a member of a team and the result accepted without bitterness or conceit.

'Played at its best, between first-class teams, football is a wonderful spectacle. I love its drama, its smooth playing skill and its long carefully laid rhythm, with the added flavour of sometimes contrasting style. And its great occasions are, for me at any rate, unequalled in the world of sport. I feel a sense of romance, wonder and mystery, a sense of beauty and a sense of poetry.

'On such occasions the game is larger than life. It has something of the timeless magical quality of legend.'

That was the philosophy Matt Busby always strove to convey to the many players who passed through his hands. He wasn't always successful of course because football is still a battle, full of frailties as well as ideals. Nevertheless there was usually something special about his teams and the great players who became legends.

He told me afterwards: 'When I was made a Freeman I felt humble because if I have done anything for Manchester it is little compared with the things Manchester did for me.'

The freedom of Manchester was just one of the many honours that came his way in recognition of his achievements. Awarded the CBE in 1958, he was knighted in June 1968, the year after being given the freedom of Manchester, and in 1972 Pope Paul VI made him a Knight Commander of St Gregory, one of the Vatican's highest honours. His retirement from the front line of management in 1970 brought an invitation to join the board of directors and soon afterwards he became the club's first president.

With the three great teams he built, Busby won five League Championships, the FA Cup twice out of four finals, saw his protégés claim the FA Youth Cup an unprecedented six times and then of course defied the realities of the Munich tragedy to become European Cup champions.

He took the trophies and honours with complete modesty and never lost his common touch. He was at ease with humble folk as well as with the famous. His players respected him as a man as well as a manager, because his authority was always wielded with courtesy and dignity.

He was essentially a straightforward man and it was often the simple things that affected him most deeply. I shall never forget the occasion in London on the morning of a match against Spurs when we were still at the hotel and the players asked him to come to one of their rooms. There they presented him with a cut glass vase to mark his twenty years as manager of United. It was such a surprise that, with emotions running high, he had to hurry out of the room to compose himself before we could mark the occasion with a photograph.

His family was always a source of inspiration to him, with his two children, Sandy and Sheena, and his grandchildren always close to him. As he happily declared when he and Lady Jean Busby celebrated their golden wedding in 1981: 'Jean has been my strength on many occasions in my life. And she is a love, a real love.'

He was a loyal caring man, too. Lady Jean died in December 1988, after a long and trying illness that eventually confined her to a nursing home. Every day Sir Matt was a visitor and even though he was no longer recognised, he was there for her.

Matt himself died in January 1994, aged eighty-four. Old Trafford was turned into a shrine as the first fans arrived at dawn to lay bouquets on the forecourt beneath the Munich clock memorial. By the end of the day there was a carpet of red and white as admirers of the grand old man of English football came with more and more flowers and to lay their scarves and flags in his memory.

From Europe came a tribute from Lennart Johansson, president of UEFA, who wrote from Berne to say: 'Sir Matt was a man of dignity, courage and warmth, who experienced both triumph and tragedy in the service of his club. He will be remembered for having built the wonderful Busby Babes team of the 1950s and who knows what that team might have achieved in European football but for the Munich air disaster in 1958, which cost so many talented young footballers their lives.

'Sir Matt himself was seriously injured in the accident, but it was a mark of his great strength of character that he survived his injuries and returned to the game he loved despite the ordeal he had suffered. Within ten years, Sir Matt had built a second great United team, which went on to win the Champions Clubs' Cup against Benfica on a night of high emotion at Wembley.

'This was perhaps Sir Matt's finest hour as a manager. His teams always embodied what is best about football, style, panache and above all entertainment. These attributes made Manchester United loved by millions throughout the world.

'After his retirement as a manager, Sir Matt continued to give valuable service not only to United but also to the European Football Union as an advisor and expert. His opinions always deserved the greatest respect. He was, quite simply, a giant of a man. Those who follow European football will never forget his achievements, and European football will be poorer with his passing. We shall all miss him.'

Sir Matt's funeral procession stopped for a few moments beside Old Trafford, which former chairman Martin Edwards believes will be a permanent memorial to his achievements as the architect of the Manchester United we know today.

'To gauge the life and work of Sir Matt you have only to look at the magnificent stadium and think back to how it was at the end of the war, bombed and derelict,' he said.

With the road beside the ground now renamed Sir Matt Busby Way, a huge bronze statue stands outside Old Trafford looking across to his adopted city of Manchester, a fitting tribute to a legend among legends.

But for all the honours and accolades heaped upon him, I think that the tribute that would have meant most to him came from one of his players. George Best led him a merry dance at times, but as Sandy Busby will tell you: 'My dad loved George.'

The feeling was mutual, as George made clear when he wrote in one of his books: 'Sir Matt became almost a father to me. I must have sorely tried his patience as a young man but he never abandoned me. The older I get, the more I appreciate what he did for me.

'He became larger than life but not to himself or to those closely associated with him. Legendary figures are often disappointing when you come to meet them, especially in football. But I have never heard anyone who has met Sir Matt disagree with the consensus, that he is an outstanding man. It isn't just the big things that he has done, but the little things that leave an imprint on another person's life.

'When I first went to Old Trafford the young lads all knew their place. We were part of the family but there was a hierarchy to be respected. We were encouraged to mix but there was never any cheeking of the elite players and there weren't any cliques, at least not until things went wrong at the end.

'This great team spirit was Sir Matt's influence and my other abiding memory of him was his capacity to remember people and things about them. For instance the first time my father went over to Old Trafford to see me play, he brought a couple of his pals with him. The next time he went to a game he had one of these friends with him again and Sir Matt not only remembered his name but where he was from and what he drank!

'One thing he wasn't though was soft, despite what many people thought about him being easy on players, especially me! I saw players go in to see him, fully determined to demand this and that and tell him exactly what they felt they were worth.

'Time after time they came out with a sheepish smile on their faces, but not feeling put down. In that respect he was tremendous. You might be called into his office for a dressing down – it happened to me on numerous occasions – and he would really get stuck into you. Then just as you were getting up to go he would wink at you.

'That's how he managed to keep everyone so happy. It was his personality and understanding and that's why I loved the guy.'

BIBLIOGRAPHY

Bobby Charlton, *My Soccer Life* (Pelham Books, 1964)

John Doherty, Ivan Ponting, *The Insider's Guide to Manchester United: Candid Profiles of Every Red Devil Since 1945* (Empire Publications, 2005)

Geoffrey Green, *There's Only One United: The Official Centenary History of Manchester United* (Hodder and Stoughton, 1978)

Harry Gregg, *Harry's Game: An Autobiography* (Mainstream Publishing, 2002)

Brian Hughes, *The Tommy Taylor Story: The Smiling Executioner* (Empire Publications, 1996)

Denis Law, *The King* (Bantam Press, 2003)

David Meek, Tom Tyrrell, *Manchester United in Europe* (Hodder and Stoughton, 2001)

David Meek, *Manchester United Greats* (Sportsprint, 1989)

David Meek (ed.), 'Legends' (Association of Former Manchester United Players, 2001–06)

Jimmy Murphy, *Matt, United and Me* (Souvenir Press Ltd, 1968)

Nobby Stiles, *After the Ball* (Hodder and Stoughton, 2003)

Frank Taylor, *The Day A Team Died* (Souvenir Press Ltd, 1983)

INDEX
